HAGARGOAR Wheatscote Univ Salem 1983

Longitude Occidentale du Meridien de Paris

On ignore si
dans cette Partie ce sont
des Terres ou des Mers

BAYE DE BAFFINS

Cercle Polaire Arctique

Tout cecy est
inconnu

MER PACIFIQUE

Tropique du Cancer

OU
Ligne Equinoctiale

ISLES SALOMON

Tropique du Capricorne

MER DU SUD

OCEAN
SEPTENTRIONAL

OCEAN

OCCIDENTAL

MER
MERIDIO

OCEAN

CARTE REDUITE
DES PARTIES CONNUES
DU GLOBE TERRESTRE
Dressée au Depost des Cartes Plans et Journaux de la Marine
POUR LE SERVICE DES VAISSEAUX DU ROY
Par Ordre de M. DE MACHAULT Garde des Sceaux de France
Ministre et Secretaire d'Etat ayant le Departement de la Marine

Par le Sr Bellin Ingenieur de la Marine et du Depost des Plans
Censeur Royal de l'Academie de Marine et de la Societe Royale de Londres

M. DCC. LV.

Cercle Polaire Antarctique

Longitude du Meridien de l Isle de Fer

Longitude Occidentale du Meridien de Paris

CAPTAIN COOK, R.N.
THE RESOLUTE MARINER

An International Record of Oceanic Discovery

Thomas Vaughan

A. A. St. C. M. Murray–Oliver

OREGON HISTORICAL SOCIETY
PORTLAND, OREGON

Printed in the U. S. A.
Graphic Arts Center
Portland, Oregon

Photographer, Maurice Hodge
Designer, Corinna Campbell Cioeta

Contents

An Appreciation

During the last 20 years I have been actively and happily involved in the wide-ranging scholarly and research oriented affairs of the most distinguished historical institution in the American West—our Oregon Historical Society.

Last year in one of our more public bursts of enthusiasm we celebrated 100 years of public service and publishing concerning all aspects of life in the North American West and the North Pacific Ocean. At the same time we recognized a new goal in enrolling our 5,000th individual member in our nonprofit learned society devoted to research and dissemination of knowledge.

After so large a commemorative program, the usual group rests and maybe even reflects. But here is our Society in its 101st year producing by far the largest international exhibition it has ever attempted. In the old days trappers were prevalent in Oregon, but they all but disappeared along with their prey.

Then the nuts and bolts of Oregon was—and it still is—its farmers—farmers of the land, of the forests, and the seas. All of us, whatever our pursuit, owe something special to the deeply inspirational and exciting story of a man, born to humble station on a rocky Scottish border farm, who rose through his great will and intellect, and by his competence "changed the face of the world."

On the eve of our American Revolution Bicentennial and in the midst of the bicentennial honoring his oceanic discoveries, I congratulate the Oregon Historical Society on this exhibition of worldwide interest to honor Captain James Cook, R.N.

TOM McCALL
Governor of Oregon

Foreword

My first close contact with the work of Captain Cook was in 1954 when, as Chief of Naval Staff of the New Zealand Navy, I made a cruise of the South Island following his explorations, and I have a photo taken as late as 1910 of Dusky Sound showing the stumps of trees cut down by his men and the rings around them made by his cables, which seemed to bring his achievements almost tangibly into the present day.

My second Cook period was in 1966 when, after retiring from the Royal Navy, I worked for the HMS Endeavour Trust, an Australian project which was going to build a replica of Cook's *Endeavour* to sail round the Horn for his bicentenary celebrations in Australia and New Zealand. This project, sadly, did not materialize but it did give me a working knowledge of his ship, of her accommodation and the alterations made by the Admiralty to fit her for her voyages.

And so it is with the greatest personal pleasure that I received the very generous invitation of the Oregon Historical Society to come to Portland to open this exhibition, and to acquaint myself with yet another area of Cook's work.

To have sailed with Captain Cook was to be brushed with the glory of Discovery. Cook, who had served before the mast as a seaman and as an apprentice in merchant ships, had such a grasp of the arts of the navigator and a mind so determined and keen that he was in fact several sorts of scientist, a writer of considerable stature and a strong commander.

As well as this, he is remembered as a great and re-sourceful leader of men; not only of his own officers and sailors but the artists and naturalists, the gentlemen and scientists who explored with him the Pacific Ocean from Arctic to Antarctic, observing and recording, to leave a splendid heritage both in art and science.

Cruising round New Zealand I felt that Cook and his scientists, botanists and artists, in a few short months had discovered 90 per cent of what we know of this country and that the rest of us have spent 200 years in filling in the rest.

It was in the pictures by painters and draughtsmen who accompanied the expeditions that the Western world found with delight new exotic regions, peopled by a savage race who at first seemed ideal for this lush paradise. The paintings of William Hodges made on Cook's Second Voyage remained unchallenged in conveying the romance of the Pacific until the work of Gauguin in our present century.

James Cook replaced speculation about the great unknown Pacific Ocean with the certainties of hydrographical survey and trained observation, and replaced myths, accumulated over the centuries, with facts.

The men of the Age of Reason saw as a justifiable end in itself the pursuit of scientific knowledge and a vast contribution was made by Cook and his fellow voyagers to man's knowledge of the shape and extent of continents and their people. Australia, New Zealand, the Pacific Islands and the western coast of North America, even to the Bering Strait, these were revealed and recorded by them in their charts, their pictures and their writings.

Cook was a man given great opportunities in the three epic voyages; his character was such that he was able to exploit them to the full. He was aware of this rôle for he wrote: "I who had the ambition not only to go farther than any man had ever been before, but as far as it was possible for man to go."

ADMIRAL SIR CHARLES MADDEN, BT, KGB
Chairman, the Board of Trustees
National Maritime Museum

Preface

The intention of the exhibition is primarily a visual and narrative description of the three great voyages, in a chronological system: But there are other components in the presentation necessary to a better understanding of the great accomplishment, the *tour de force* represented especially by the events in the last 15 years of Cook's life.

The theme then shows the rise of a Scottish plowman's son to the high pinnacle of what we must judge as everlasting world renown. The theme attempts to show how this meteoric rise was not only Cook's great doing, but also that of those many patrons, supporters and fellow mariners great and small who helped Cook make his luck.

There is a happy kind of combination of the right man at the right time who, given advantages and adversities, seems in his levelheaded and reasonable manner to turn it all usefully. So the rise from humble station to a high place in universal estimation is a paramount theme in our presentation. Joined with solid basic training, determination and eminently sensible nature is that special quality of boldness which, as Goethe later said, "has power, magic and genius in it."

Despite his personal reserve and his *sangfroid habituel* in the storm-blast and lonely watches, in the immensity of the oceans he cleaved, there may have been some times when the quiet man, Captain James Cook, must have thought back through the events of his life with some joy. He may have experienced this, as Thomas Hobbes earlier wrote in *Leviathan,* as "joy, arising from imagination of a man's own power and ability. . . that exultation of a mind called glorying."

In his memorable and many measurable accomplishments, modest, self-effacing Cook must have experienced a sense of "glorying." That he and his many associates, generous patrons and devoted followers could have achieved so much permanently useful and good is the theme of this exhibition.

THOMAS VAUGHAN
Executive Director
Oregon Historical Society

Acknowledgements

This kind of record-catalog could never have been established had it not been for the faithful and inspired scholarship of
PROFESSOR J. C. BEAGLEHOLE, OM
to whom all our sincere thanks and admiration are given. He was *the* Cook scholar.

TJGV
AASt. CMM-O

Consultants to the Exhibition
Leslie Boas, London
B. T. Carter, National Maritime Museum, London
Hon. Merritt Cootes, Florence
B. A. L. Cranstone, Museum of Mankind, British Museum
E. A. P. Crownhart-Vaughan, Portland
Lt. Cdr. A. C. F. David, R.N., Taunton, England
R. L. Dean, Consul General, Australia
Russell Doust, Sydney, Australia
Donald G. Ellis, Christchurch, New Zealand
Mable Erie, Portland
Col. M. J. P. d'Ermengard, Portland
Mrs. Pauline Fanning, Canberra, Australia
Peter Gathercole, Cambridge University, England
Robin Gibson, National Portrait Gallery, London
Max Hope, Consul General, New Zealand
Adrienne Kaeppler, Honolulu
Priscilla Knuth, Portland
P. J. Lawler, Australia

Roza G. Liapunova, Leningrad
Marquis of Lothian, London
Robert Monroe, University of Washington Library
Mrs. Suzanne Mourot, Sydney, Australia
John Munday, National Maritime Museum, London
Robert Oliver, Salem, Oregon
Sydney Parker, National Maritime Museum, London
Sir James Plymsol, Australian Ambassador (presently to U.S.S.R.)
Frank Quinlan, ARBC State of Oregon
Miss Verda Roy, Hulihee Palace, Hawaii
Erna V. Siebert, Leningrad
Jane Silverman, Honolulu
John Steelquist, M.D., San Jose, California
A. A. Stepanov, Khabarovsk, Siberia
J. Herbert Stone, Oregon Geographic Names, Portland
Mrs. Mary Helen Styan, Regent, Queen Emma Summer Palace, Honolulu
James Traue, Wellington, New Zealand
Dr. Helen Wallis, Keeper of the Map Room, British Museum, London
William Wessinger, Oregon Geographic Names
Walter Muir Whitehill, North Andover, Massachusetts
Jean Whyte, Canberra, Australia
Rudie Wilhelm, Jr., Portland
B. K. Williams, London
Ross Wurm, Modesto, California
T. C. Price Zimmermann, Portland
The Entire Staff of the Oregon Historical Society

Lenders

Other museums, libraries, archives and individuals contributing to the Exhibition most generously:

Australia
National Library of Australia, Canberra
National Library of New South Wales, Sydney
Australasian Pioneers Club, Sydney

Great Britain
Lords Commissioners, The Admiralty
National Maritime Museum, Greenwich
National Portrait Gallery, London
The British Museum, London — including Museum of Mankind
University Museum of Archaeology and Ethnology, Cambridge
Ministry of Defense, Hydrographic Department (Navy), Taunton
Royal Art Academy, London
Royal Society, Royal Science Museum, London
The Library, Windsor Castle, Berkshire

New Zealand
Government House, Wellington
Alexander Turnbull Library, Wellington
National Museum, Wellington
Hocken Library, University of Otago, Dunedin
Auckland City Art Gallery, Auckland
Auckland Public Library (Sir George Grey Collection)
Bishop Suter Art Gallery, Nelson
Sir Alister McIntosh, KGMG, Wellington

United States
Academy of Natural Sciences, Philadelphia, Pennsylvania
Daughters of Hawaii at Hulihee Palace, Kailua-Kona, Hawaii
Franklin Institute, Philadelphia, Pennsylvania
Los Angeles County Museum of Art, Los Angeles, California
Mariners Museum, Newport News, Virginia
Newport Historical Society, Newport, Rhode Island
Oregon Historical Society, Portland, Oregon
University of Washington, Seattle, Washington

U. S. S. R.
Milukho-Maklay Institute of Ethnography, Moscow
Museum of Anthropology and Ethnography, Leningrad
The Academy of Sciences, Moscow and Leningrad
The Presidium, Moscow

Canada
The Public Archives of Canada, Ottawa, Ontario

Ireland
The National Museum of Ireland, Dublin

Introduction

In 1968 Thomas Vaughan, Director of the Oregon Historical Society, was working in the magnificent library collections of the National Maritime Museum, Greenwich. The naval museum on the Thames had just completed installation of a superb gallery devoted to Captain Cook and his voyages, one that would attract worldwide interest.

The Cook Gallery was again visited in 1970 together with the vast holdings of the British Museum whose Cook drawings, manuscripts and ethnographical pieces the Director had studied in 1961.

Time passed and by 1973 plans were underway in many parts of the United States and Great Britain, too, to appropriately commemorate the American Revolution Bicentennial. What better idea than to fittingly memorialize the events of the Bicentennial era in company with the Cook bicentenary recognitions? Sir James McDonald, KBE, our distinguished British Consul in Portland, was approached, and as so often through the years, his response was immediate and substantial. A major maritime exhibition honoring Cook was logical and compelling.

The explorations of the great navigator along the Oregon coast in 1778 were exceedingly important to the mercantile prospects of this region. Immediately upon his finding report, a large-scale trade in furs was initiated by English, European and American trading vessels pursuing sea otter furs and other desirable pelts. The second voyage of Boston-based Captain Gray, in the *Columbia Rediviva,* is our prime example of American trade and discovery, for, in 1792, he penetrated, at last, the elusive Columbia River mouth—the River of the West.

Working in cooperation with the Marquis of Lothian, Chairman of the British Liaison Committee, as well as Mrs. Ernestine Carter, OBE, Sir Patrick Dean, GCMG and Lady Dean, Lord Gore-Booth, GCMG, KCVO, and Rt. Hon. Lord Harlech, PC, KCMG, the suggestion of an exhibition was passed through the interested Director of the U.S. Bicentennial Secretariat, Mr. Leslie Boas, to the vigorous director of the National Maritime Museum, Mr. Basil Greenhill, CMG. Sir James McDonald stated that if a substantial loan of prized Cook memorabilia could be made it would provide a strong incentive for other countries to make loans of their national treasures to further enrich the magnificent plan envisaged. The busy museum Director may have been taken aback by the magnitude of the proposal advanced by Sir James and Mr. Boas, but at least he did not say no.

With the added support of Mr. Aubrey Morgan, CMG, former Counselor and Personal Assistant to Sir Oliver Franks and Sir Roy Makins (British Ambassadors to the United States) and wartime Director General of British Information Services in America, Director Vaughan again approached the Greenwich officials, including Mr. John Munday. After extensive personal negotiations a general agreement was concluded whereby the Museum would send over its major Cook treasures in a fortuitous time when the Captain Cook Gallery was being remodeled, the agreement pursuant to receiving assurances that other countries would participate to the limit of their abilities.

I want to comment, then, on the exceptionally generous response from Australia and New Zealand, especially through the Australian Ambassador, Sir James Plymsol and Consul General Roger L. Dean in San Francisco, and the immediate and energetic support and advice of Mr. Max Hope, New Zealand Consul General, San Francisco. There followed an enthusiastic response from the U.S.S.R. where Director Vaughan had uncovered the little known Cook treasures of the Third Voyage received by Major von Behm from the *Resolution* via Petropavlovsk while serving as Commandant of Kamchatka in the 1770s. These early ethnographical treasures had been dispatched overland to Catherine the Great across Siberia and the Urals.

A special Cook Exhibition Committee was immediately formed in the Society, which President Moe Tonkon asked me to serve as Chairman. The Committee included the aforesaid Sir James McDonald and Aubrey Morgan as well as Museum Committee Chairman Jane Stimson Miller and former Society president, John Youell. All members had had experience tracking the great explorer in the South Pacific Islands, in New Zealand or Australia, as well as along the Oregon and Washington coasts, and north to Nootka Sound. Director Vaughan continued to serve as General Planner while Associate Director Millard McClung was appointed Exhibit Coordinator. Very soon he was flying the Southern Cross at Wellington, Canberra and other museum locations.

Further contacts were made with museums in Austria, Ireland, Germany (East and West), Italy, Canada, Scotland, Switzerland, South Africa (Capetown), Sweden, and of course museums and learned societies of the United States. The exhibition was then assured, but with an accelerated date: to begin July 1, 1974 and run through January 1, 1975.

Our Captain Cook Exhibit Committee was most anxious, from the very start, to have an exhibit catalog prepared which would adequately outline the voyages and their background and contain the important descriptive lists necessary to the record of this singular exhibit. And yet we wished the book to have a life of its own beyond 1975. Under the able direction of Thomas Vaughan this book took shape, with very special thanks to the skilled assistance of A. A. St. C. M. Murray-Oliver who came from New Zealand to assist this complex project. We are most grateful to Prime Minister the Right Hon. Norman Kirk for designating this brilliant Cook scholar as New Zealand Special Coordinator for the Exhibition and releasing him from his duties as Education Officer of the Turnbull Library in Wellington, New Zealand.

EDMUND HAYES
Chairman, Cook Exhibition Committee
Oregon Historical Society
July 1, 1974

Abbreviations

ACAG Auckland City Art Gallery, Auckland, New Zealand

AM Sir Alister McIntosh, KCMG, Wellington, New Zealand

ANS Academy of Natural Sciences, Philadelphia, Pennsylvania

APL Auckland Public Library, Auckland, New Zealand

ATL Alexander Turnbull Library, Wellington, New Zealand

BML British Museum, London, England

BSG Bishop Suter Art Gallery, Nelson, New Zealand

CAM University Museum of Archaeology and Ethnology, Cambridge, England

DGE Donald G. Ellis, Christchurch, New Zealand

FIS Franklin Institute Science Museum, Philadelphia, Pennsylvania

GH Government House, Wellington, New Zealand

HL Hocken Library, University of Otago, Dunedin, New Zealand

LEN Museum of Anthropology and Ethnography, Leningrad, USSR

LNSW Library of New South Wales, Sydney, NSW Australia

LACMA Los Angeles County Museum of Art, Los Angeles, California

MM Mariners Museum, Newport News, Virginia

NLA National Library of Australia, Canberra, Australia

NMG National Maritime Museum, Greenwich, London, England

NMI National Museum of Ireland, Dublin, Ireland

NMW National Museum of New Zealand, Wellington, New Zealand

NPL National Portrait Gallery, London, England

OHS Oregon Historical Society, Portland, Oregon

PAC Public Archives of Canada, Ottawa, Canada

UWS University of Washington, Seattle, Washington

WC The Library, Windsor Castle, Berkshire

EARLY PACIFIC VOYAGES

Thomas Vaughan

Sir Peter Medawar, the brilliant Nobel prizewinner in biology, in a reference suggested that before Columbus set sail across the Atlantic the coat of arms of the royal family of Spain had been an *impressa,* depicting the Pillars of Hercules (or Straits of Gibraltar) with the motto *Ne Plus Ultra.* In the 15th century Spain was the outpost of the great Mediterranean world and there was "no more beyond." To the west it was, including by inference all islands including the British, a void.

But when Columbus returned with the news of his great discovery the Spanish throne thriftily did the one necessary thing. The *Ne* was erased, leaving the Pillars of Hercules in the positive bearing the motto, *Plus Ultra.* There was more beyond . . . And so this condition remained unresolved through almost 300 years. There was more, but what?

Operating on the dynamic theory the English had from the exuberant times of Raleigh, Drake, Frobisher and Elizabeth accepted, consciously or otherwise, Francis Bacon's deep statement that "the end of our foundation is the knowledge of causes and the secret motion of things; and the enlarging of the bounds of human empire, to the effecting of all things possible." The pragmatic statesman may have had mankind's thought in mind rather than geographical boundaries. But through the succeeding 200 years British adventurers, soldiers and statesmen had a glorious run.

Their concentration however was in the reaches of the Atlantic and Indian oceans, and their meandering sounds and bays. Aside from Drake's magnificent accomplishment in the *Pelican* turned *Golden Hind,* few Englishmen had cruised the Pacific. But in the mid-18th century this situation gradually and then swiftly changed. As usual there was among several factors a very critical competitive aspect. Among competing imperial expansionists the English had emerged on top, effectually blocking their greatest competitor, France. Withdrawing reluctantly from Quebec and Montreal, from Dominica and St. Lucia in the West Indies, from Martinique, as well as Pondicherry on the Indian subcontinent, France almost inevitably followed the Spanish and Dutch through the tortuous reefs of the Moluccas which had for generations guarded the privileged trading stations scattered through the straits and islands of the legendary East.

Through the centuries few Englishmen had found their way into the labyrinth, and almost all other merchant-adventurers had their hands full and their pockets filled along the continental shoreline north to fabled Cathay and Cipango, the Japanese islands.

The vastness of the Pacific had been shaped and explored through centuries, from the endless and unrecorded voyages of windblown Micronesians to the time the Portuguese pilot Magellan sailed for Spain in the 16th century. It was this period when the Spanish dynamic was most magnificent and the Hapsburg armadas impressive in every sea.

Balboa moving down from the infested jungle of the Panamanian hills had sighted the blue of Mar del Zur and claimed it for Spain. Magellan searching for the Spice Islands—the Moluccas—had left Seville with five ships in August, 1519 and coasted down South America to meet the blinding snow and 40-foot tides of the rock-filled water known today as the Straits of Magellan. One can understand how the "other sea" when at last reached, might have been called the Pacific. On this first voyage it was as the Russians say, "the quiet ocean."

A large part of Magellan's men were drowned or killed or died of scurvy. One ship returned home to Spain to record the first European circumnavigation. The *Victoria's* voyage lasted three years and Magellan's bones were left to bleach on an unimportant Philippine island.

Mendoza discovered the Solomon Islands in 1568, and Pedro Quiros sailing for Portugal believed these islands guarded the great continent which most sailors felt must lie to the south. Quiros left the Peruvian coast December, 1605 with a second ship commanded by Luis Vaez de Torres. The following May, plagued by scurvy, he sighted and claimed land which they believed to be part of the Southern Continent. He named it Australia de Espiritu Santo. He had found the New Hebrides.

Quiros returned east to Acapulco and Peru and Madrid. Torres sailed west passing through the reefs guarding the strait between New Guinea and the real Australian continent. While the hazardous passage today bears his name, his feat was for many years forgotten and his report lay unanswered and unrecognized by the Spanish monarchs, increasingly preoccupied with European and ecclesiastical affairs.

During this tumultous internecine period the Dutch were trying to break the Spanish vise on the Netherlands. During their war for independence Spanish and Portuguese ports were naturally closed to Dutch merchants and traders. But they had already begun to move through the Indian Ocean to the Indies. Finding a favorable response, the Dutch East Indian Company was formed in 1602. More interested in trade than exploration, the Dutch nonetheless made some noteworthy discoveries as they branched south from ports of the Indies. What they gradually found and described was the barren, savage infested shoreline of New Holland —the north shore of Australia.

Following orders from Governor General Anthony Van Diemen of the Company, Captain Abel Tasman sailed from Batavia in 1642 on a southern sweep. Reaching distant southerly latitudes without sighting any land, he turned east and ran into Van Diemen's land, now called Tasmania, and then the South Island of New Zealand which he did not distinguish as separated from New Holland. Returning to Batavia he set out again in 1644, but failed to find anything comparable to the unrewarding islands earlier encountered. The Dutch withdrew to interior lines and profitable enterprises in the north toward Japan.

We know the details of Captain Francis Drake and the *Pelican* turned *Golden Hind*. He had returned from the first English circumnavigation in 1580, loaded with Spanish treasure from the Peruvian coast. Despite his magnificent achievement and reward from an expedition essentially for plunder, few English had subsequently penetrated the Pacific. More than a century elapsed before another Englishman achieved record— William Dampier, the fabulous but erratic pirate-explorer who saw Australia as well as New Guinea and the Galapagos Islands.

In the meantime much had transpired: first in the means of accurate and dependable navigation, and second in European and imperial warfare. Huge advances had been made in the arts associated with hydrography—in navigation, geodesy, astronomy, bathymetrics, chart-making, and formalized record keeping. The real shape of the earth had been at last determined and latitudes established with the equator at 0° and poles at 90°.

While meridian lines were being purposefully established in the great capitals of the expanding nations, by 1765 it was finally determined that for the British the meridian point for all calculations on land or sea would be the Royal Observatory at Greenwich (GMT) where Isaac Newton had once exercised his genius. Eventually this point, extended to an imaginary line and lines running in all measurable directions from longitude 0°, was accepted by scientists everywhere as the standard meridian.

In the same era there were also lunar calculations using the cycles and phases of the moon, and fixed tables established for calculation. A person of Cook's brilliance, or of Green his astronomer on the First Voyage, could determine the lunar fixes, but most could not. Too, the moon was and is uncertain and clouds and blizzards could obscure it for days on end. This meant that the longitude or east-west position from Greenwich could become free-floating until the moon was again perceived and fixed.

The coast and geodetic surveys of today have much of the land mass established and the mystery neutralized, but in the 18th and earlier centuries land, including reefs and shoals, might appear out of the fog at any time—or not be perceived but rather heard as the keel crunched on a reef or bar or the bottom disintegrated in the surf and foam of a dark night. It is often noted that Cook had an uncanny faculty for appearing on deck suddenly and ordering a turn—violent or gradual. Only later would the coral island, reef, or emerald ice barrier appear to others. While his sixth sense was involved, some of this seeming clairvoyance was due to his accomplishment as a master hydrographer who understood how water, especially ocean water, behaves. But there are very few Wallises, Clerkes, and Cooks to sense, sometimes too late, how waves mass and change their shape, how sea waters course in the "roaring forties" with no land to impede their flow around the globe, or how water color changes with fluctuating depths.

It was during this period in time, the mid-18th century, the English entry into the great Pacific Ocean, that intense work was being carried forward to establish the movement of ships of whatever size in relationship to space (the vast oceans) and time, the clock gradually established by thinkers and mechanics through the centuries.

In the 18th century some governments including the British, had begun to offer prizes for an accurate and dependable time-keeper: the British Board of Longitude establishing their prize at 20,000 pounds, a great sum in 1714—and in 1770 when the prize still lay unclaimed.

The hardnosed Board members demanded a chronometer which would, under any circumstances, in heat, storm or blizzard, on land or sea, exactly, at all times, report Greenwich time "at the end of a six weeks voyage, within 60 geographical miles, £10,000, within 40 miles, £15,000, within 30 miles, £20,000." The first person to meet this stipulation, and better it, was the sourly treated genius, John Harrison. Eventually he made four timepieces that could be duplicated by others,

as Larcum Kendall precisely did the fourth. It was of this Harrison-Kendall piece, still ticking in Greenwich today, that Cook said on the Second Voyage: "I must here take notice that our longitude can never be erroneous while we have so good a guide as Mr. Kendall's watch." And so it was because of these great instrumental advances that Anson, Carteret, Wallis and Cook could set sail with great assurance. Their "sloping masts and dipping prows" moved toward the hot and copper skies and the Auroras—Australis and Borealis.

What was this new drive? The British had achieved ascendancy in the Atlantic and were busy devouring and trading their rich prizes while ignoring the colonials who had helped secure them. Britain was supreme at sea, but there were many parts beyond the capes unknown, uncharted and unoccupied. It would not do to have lands yet unexplored occupied by the recently defeated French or the Spanish. True, the British fleet could take on their flotillas combined, and just about any other combination, but the possession of rich, new Pacific discoveries could change the balance. And as happened ordinarily following wars, the urge to discovery had been stimulated. There was a special stimulus in the observed fact that the Spanish, fortifying Juan Fernandez beyond Cape Horn, worked to keep "their Pacific" closed. And France, through her great soldier turned sailor, Bougainville, wished to replace lost Atlantic possessions with discoveries in the Pacific, starting with a staging platform in the South Atlantic Falkland Islands. This naturally spurred the Admiralty, already digesting news of Commodore Anson's discoveries and anticipating those of Byron, Carteret and Wallis. They had already prepared for another long voyage of exploration, reacting perhaps to the prod of one of their number, Piercy Brett (who had served with Anson in *Centurion*). They had purchased a ship even before they selected a commander—a cat-built Whitby bark. The Pacific stage was set.

In *The Advancement of Learning* (1604) the profound Bacon states that "Just history is of three kinds, with regard to the three objects it designs to represent; which are either a portion of time, a memorable person, or an illustrious action." This finely drawn observation is especially appropriate to James Cook.

THE VOYAGES OF
CAPTAIN COOK

Thomas Vaughan

Two years before Cook's First Voyage the first edition of the *Nautical Almanac* was published with tables to determine the longitudes, a position on the earth's surface east or west of Greenwich. Carrying through with these improved studies, Cook and Green made studies on their passage around the Horn. Through several observations of the sun and moon, using Hadley's reflecting quadrants and the also newly devised sextant, and a solid pocket watch, they straightened out the latitude and accurately plotted the longitude of the Cape. Through that treacherous passage Cook laid out a passage for the earlier discovered Tahiti. On the long voyage he concentrated on diet and exercise for the crew and his gentleman passengers. We know that when they arrived in Tahiti the men were in good health. The quadrant for taking the most necessary measurement of Venus was not as successful, since the refractive effects caused by the atmosphere of Venus prevented precise observations (this was true of observations taken throughout the world). The passage was somewhat unsuccessfully observed, and notes about the breadfruit tree, the island staff of life, taken.

After three perhaps idyllic months in Tahiti, the ship "steer'd to the southward in search of the so much before talked of Southern Continent." Following the precise and pointed Secret Instructions concerning discovery which would "rebound greatly to the honour of this nation as a Maritime Power as well as to the dignity of the Crown of Great Britain," the *Endeavour* moved out of the tropics down to the 40° parallel. Sighting nothing, Cook "steer'd to the westward between the latitude of 30° and 40° until we fell in with the East Coast of New Zealand a very small part of the west coast of which was first discovered [by] Tasman in 1642, but he never once set foot upon it, this country was thought to be a part of the Southern Continent, but I found it to be two large Islands, both of which I circumnavigated in a space of Six Months, they are together nearly as big as Great Britain." (A letter to John Walker, 13 September 1771).

Leaving New Zealand they sailed toward New Holland (Australia) on April 1, 1770. Caught by the prevailing winds they eventually made landfall not at Van Dieman's Land as Cook intended, but at 38° south on the Australian coast. Cook named the southernmost point of land after Lieutenant Hicks because he "was the first who discovered this land." The quiet and observing Hicks who was so useful to Cook died on the passage home from murderous Batavia.

Botany Bay was found and thoroughly recorded by Cook, Banks, and Solander. Upon departure they ground *Endeavour's* keel on the Great Barrier Reef and eventually found their way to Dutch Batavia where a thorough overhaul was made. Unfortunately, during this 10-week shoreside repair various virulent and lethal germs and diseases were contracted by Cook's formerly healthy crew. Eventually 30 were taken from the rolls.

The unique record of good health established prior to Batavia must be attributed to Cook and the special diet he provided the men eventually at every station. This included sauerkraut, portable soup and malt, plus exercise and clean clothes. In other words, personal hygiene, which was never mentioned in the reports of earlier voyages.

When at length Cook returned from his long journey and Banks had dropped over the side early to mesmerize London society with his tales, Cook could report to the Admiralty Board.

And upon your arrival in England you are immediately to repair to this office in order to lay before us a full account of your proceedings in the whole course of your voyage, taking care before you leave the vessel to demand from the Officers and Petty Officers the log books and journals they may have kept, and to seal them up for our inspection, and enjoining them, and the whole crew not to divulge where they have been until they shall have permission so to do.

Another great explorer in the North Pacific Ocean a generation earlier is said to have referred to Horace for his favorite motto: "Tu, nisi ventis/Debes lidibrium cave." "Unless thou wouldst see thy craft the sport of winds, beware." And in some ways Cook was approaching his most dangerous voyage, more so than the stormy reefs off Whitby and the fogbound mouth of the Thames or the rocky bays of Newfoundland.

It is best that some great men never go near a town and its labyrinthine ways, especially a great imperial city like London, full of grasping men and the wreckage of many large dreams. But again Cook reveals his eminent sensibility and control. He could not have been anything but rankled at Banks carrying on about "his voyage," but the Lieutenant kept his head throughout. And what a scene it must have been, as he reported, without fuss or flamboyance to the Lords Admiralty on what they had asked him to do and how he had discharged their instructions—to the hilt and far beyond.

In a way one can reasonably wonder how he got the perfect vessel in the first place, and how he got the assignment—there were plenty of others high above him in military and social preferment. But after his wondrous return home there was little question in professional circles. Cook was the man. His competence continued "to change the face of the world." And he had brought almost everyone home with him excepting some who were sick when they started and those burned out by Batavia. Their Lordships "extremely well approved . . ."

Throughout his stay in London at his new house at Mile End in Old Town, Cook conducted himself most circumspectly. So much so, we regret to say, that while everyone mentions him no one notes particulars about him. Away from his ships and thanks perhaps to the great quantity of "personal letters" Mrs. Cook threw away, we know very little of what transpired, other than that he was very well received everywhere—and warmly by King George who had, a few days earlier, received the enthusiastic Banks.

Cook seemed as "adaptable," as Beaglehole observed to the Royal Society in June of 1969, on land as on sea. He seemed happy and very much at ease with his friends, fellow Yorkshireman Palliser, now Comptroller of the Navy; Sir John Williams, Surveyor of the Navy; and John Montagu, 4th Earl of Sandwich and, more to the point, First Sea Lord. It was men of this talent, prescience and power with whom Cook worked in planning the Second Voyage to the South Seas and the great unknown continent. Aside from the oft mentioned and regrettable fantasizing of Banks and the housing of his retinue, the plans were superb.

Perhaps through good fortune the *Endeavour* was sent off to the Falkland Islands on another assignment and the *Resolution* and *Adventure* chosen—two more colliers. What better? The complement of the flagship was 117 officers and men, and of her consort 81. At the offset there were several desertions among those who resisted the idea of a long voyage, even with "the great navigator," but eventually the rolls were filled. On *Resolution*, 18 of the men were marines including a lieutenant and a sergeant; on *Adventure*, 12 were marines, including a 2nd lieutenant.

Among others signed on when Banks withdrew his wonderful entourage in a huff, were Johann R. Forster and his 17-year-old son Georg (who would die under the Paris guillotine); William Hodges, the official yet inspired artist; steady and reserved William Wales and William Bayly, astronomers. They sailed from Plymouth 13 July 1772 with *Adventure* under the command of Captain Tobias Furneaux. He had sailed as a lieutenant with Wallis and had enormous experience backed up by modest imagination and personal initiative.

They left the Cape of Good Hope and by January 1773 had crossed the Antarctic Circle and met the ice barrier thrusting out from the still unperceived continent 75 miles to the south. The ships parted and met again in Queen Charlotte Sound, New Zealand. They sailed to Tahiti to recover themselves. When Cook returned to Queen Charlotte Sound to prepare for a second assault on the Antarctic he lost Furneaux and *Adventure*. They eventually preceded him home. Cook sailed south alone and spent ". . . near 4 months beating about between the latitude 48° and 68° and once I got as high as 71° 10′ and farther it was not possible to go for ice which lay as firm as land," as he wrote to John Walker, his old Quaker friend and collier owner in Whitby. And later he wrote in his journal the famous words: ". . . I, whose ambition leads me not only further than any other man has been before me, but as far as I think it possible for man to go, was not sorry to meet this interruption . . ."

Cook again returned to his favorite Tahiti where he witnessed the singular sight of an estimated 8,000 men decked out for battle in their war canoes. It was just as well he had returned for the Antarctic extremities had caused great physical stress, even to the Commander who suffered severely from painful colic. It may have been an ulcer. Despite his physical pain he had sighted Easter Island, noted Fatu Haku, and many other islands which with his instruments and charts he "made solid." From Tahiti Cook returned to Tonga and then moved on to landings at the New Hebrides, New Caledonia and Norfolk Island (see drawings).

As one can see, some of the landings were attended by tense moments and savage outbursts—on both sides. There were also the usual number of ragged reefs, sudden squalls, loss of wind and unexpected currents demanding, as always, Cook's deepest skills and prudence. This greatest voyage of all time proceeded in the direction of Australia and New Zealand and then again into the Antarctic, crossing the Circle five times! When he finally returned to Table Bay, Cape Town, he was shocked to discover that Furneaux had preceded him there by 12 months. He was further shocked to learn that New Zealanders (Maoris) with whom he had recently palavered, had earlier eaten 10 of Furneaux's crew on a

shore expedition commanded by a gun-happy coxswain who had laid down his musket for lunch. A very bad exchange.

Cook spent five weeks reconditioning. He sent on by the *Ceres* Indiaman charts and information to the Admiralty including several of Hodges' drawings and a great tribute for Larcum Kendal: "Mr. Kendal's Watch has exceeded expectations of its most Zealous advocates." Unfortunately, he also read editor Hawkesworth's account of his First Voyage and he was scandalized at the many errors made. He left the Cape on 27 April to the accompaniment of a Danish band and saluting cannoneers.

On the 15th of May he anchored at St. Helena and there met the governor who proved to be John Skottowe, the son of Thomas Skottowe who had been responsible for Cook's first schooling on his rocky Yorkshire farm!

On the 19th they raised Fayal Island in the Azores and after five days departed for Plymouth and Spithead where he arrived on July 30. "Having been absent from England Three Years and Eighteen Days, in which time I lost but four men and one only of them by sickness." And Furneaux had added one man, Omai of Huahine who would be painted by Reynolds, Dance, and Hodges and captivate London.

On July 31, Solander reported from the Admiralty, ". . . Capt. Cook is arrived. I have not had an opportunity of conversing with him, as he is still in the board-room—giving an account of himself and Co." And again it would be (as Beaglehole so nicely stated in quoting Robert Bridges' *Testament of Beauty*) the fact that "wisdom lies in masterful administration of the unforeseen." He had sailed more than 60,000 miles.

Cook dined at the Mitre with Fellows of the Royal Society. He was received by the King, given a fine sinecure at Greenwich Hospital and at last made a Fellow of the Royal Society with extraordinary backing. He presented a widely acclaimed paper on the health of seamen and had a long conversation with James Boswell. One could only wish there had been more of them, and that perhaps Boswell might have gone along on the Third Voyage as he suggested to Samuel Johnson. One did have that sort of inclination, he said, "till one considers how very little one learns!" But later Doctor Johnson confessed that he too wished to go, and only his infirmities prevented him. In the E.G.R. Taylor Memorial Lecture (1968, London), Beaglehole stresses how regrettable it is that Boswell did not go, and how likely it is that Cook would have soon thrown him overboard, along with his notebook. But our insights might have been richer.

The esteemed navigator was also appointed post-captain in the *Kent* (74), and painted by Nathaniel Dance. He was also obliged to take issue with Forster pére who was, as usual, unreasonable, argumentative, arrogant and unfair. And Mrs. Cook was thinking of having another son. Along with all other matters Cook had been inveigled into preparing for a Third Voyage (to the North Pacific) and he was selecting ships—unfortunately the worn *Resolution,* as tired as he. But having forever laid to rest the question of a great southern continent, it now seemed almost inevitable that he would be sent to solve the last riddle, one 300 years old—the elusive but surely existing Northwest Passage. Parliament had offered £20,000 to the man first discovering it. Or maybe there was a Northeast Passage, also something to keep in mind.

Perhaps Cook found Samuel Johnson's great city a bit too distracting; perhaps he was ill at ease away from his true home which by now might well have become the South Pacific. True, he would receive no Copley Gold Medal there nor would King George and the great seek him out for an opinion; but one might suppose his mind, which may have tilted just a bit, was most at home on shipboard—his ship, with his men. Urgent as some may have supposed the Northwest Passage search to be, Cook's almost hasty departure must be brooded over. Sensible as he always was, one has to think about his almost urgent leave-taking and the condition of *Resolution.*

What was going on in the great naval yards of England at that time on the very eve of a colonial war? What were the distractions that would have prevented the ever so careful Commander of the Second Voyage from fully assessing the capabilities of his almost legendary ship for a third perhaps larger undertaking? We can only suppose. *Resolution* left Plymouth on 11

July 1776 one week after the Declaration of Independence was announced in Philadelphia.

Within days the once staunch vessel began to leak due to bad caulking. After stopping on Tenerife in the Azores for wine and repairs he headed again for Capetown for a heralded fourth visit. Sailing with him were a number of young men—in fact the larger part were in their twenties or younger, and several such as Portlock, Dixon and gifted George Vancouver, would carve their own place in the explorers' realm. Others would gain fame in other ways, timeless or fleeting; Rice as a Captain of Nelson killed at Copenhagen and James Trevenen with the Russians at Vyborg.

More lasting is the contribution of Cambridgian William Ellis, a surgeon's mate who has given us meticulous and presentable watercolors. The great work, of course, is that of 23-year-old John Webber of Switzerland, who will be forever remembered by his voluminous output and meticulous artistic record. To him and to the chartmakers we shall always be grateful, and to Gore, too, for eventually getting them home with the help of another chartmaker and draftsman, the already opinionated William Bligh, ship master of *Resolution* at 21. With only six years' experience in sailing, one must wonder if the Navy was not stretched very thin in choosing Bligh. One must also mention Gore's second, James King, a person the ordinarily reserved Cook took to immediately as he did to the doomed surgeon, William Anderson, who would die while *Resolution* traversed the Aleutians. And lost in a too brief notice of the crews the wonderful companion of three voyages, Captain Charles Clerke who commanded *Discovery,* a new collier type carrying 70 men, 8 four-pounders, 8 swivels, and 8 musquetows. Clerke, already carrying the seeds of tuberculosis from his stay in Fleet Street prison as security for his brother's debts, would die and be buried in the "solemn waste prospect" of Petropavlovsk. Perhaps only King, the intellect of the group, would have so described the bleak Siberian waste. But later on Samwell, Anderson's assistant who "gloried" in Cook, said: ". . . there never was a Collection of fine lads take us for all in all, got together as there was in the *Resolution & Discovery.*"

When all repairs and victualing and animals were

gathered for sailing and the *Discovery* joined, Cook left Capetown on November 30 bound again for Queen Charlotte Sound and to be sure of more information about the cannibal luncheon. On the way they stopped at Kerguelen Island and Christmas Harbor which retains its Kerguelen given name, Boie de l'Oiseau. At Van Diemen's Land (Tasmania) the foretop mast and its main topgallant mast came down on the deck with all its rigging in a maze. In Queen Charlotte Sound and Grassy Cove, Cook had at last the leader of the cannibal murderers for close questioning in *Resolution's* great cabin. Having determined the facts Cook let Kaheua go, to the chagrin of several including Omai.

In the Tonga Islands was the finest dancing the men ever witnessed amidst designs of dark treachery just short of execution. With the cattle well fed and the winds changed at last, the ships moved on to Tahiti which they reached in August. In November Omai left Cook at Huahine with his two native companions from Tonga. He wept as he left and his years on the island were to be few. Leaving the Society Islands so well described through three voyages, Cook, in December, proceeded north toward New Albion and Drake's Claim. In this way, on December 24, he encountered Christmas Island. After filling up with 300 sea turtles on the bare 300,000-acre island, they moved northwest on January 2.

It was an altogether unexpected event when on the 18th high land was observed to the north. One of Cook's greatest discoveries was in view. On the 19th he stood off Kauai to the north, one of the major islands in the group he named for Sandwich, his great patron, but which we ordinarily call the Hawaiian Islands: ". . . a Groupe of Islands inhabited by the same nation as Otaheite (the Tahitians) and abounding with hogs and roots." The islanders were obviously highly structured in a caste system, but when they saw Cook approach they all prostrated themselves. This may have affected the great navigator's sense of proportion, but much more distracting were the several days he spent trying to get a safe anchorage off the islands, making various trades for foodstuffs, and determining that, through the laws of wind and chance, no European had ever visited the islands. It would appear to him and

to our own anthropologists that the natives had been cut off from any contact with the outside world for perhaps several hundred years. The Spanish sailing from Manila to Acapulco passed miles to the north.

Cook, pushing on toward the North American coast, fell in with Drake's New Albion at about 45° on the Oregon shore. For some days he tacked back and forth in the wind and drizzle. King remarked on the fact that there had been no advance notice, that they were ". . . almost free from any indications of our approaching so great a Continent . . ." And on the 7th of February Cook recorded a five-mile-long, 1,000-foot rocky face promontory, Cape Foulweather, which name it bears today—and he correctly noted it at 44° 50′ N.

On Wednesday, the 11th, he named Cape Perpetua for the special fact that he had also seen it on the 7th. He also noted Cape Arago, which on his southern tack we believe he named Cape Gregory. On March 13, at his southernmost point he stood off to the north, naming Cape Flattery on March 22 while, in the storm and darkness, missing the entrance to the Strait of Juan de Fuca and Puget Sound.

Then on the 30th Lieutenant King went in with three armed boats on the coast of Vancouver Island followed by Cook in a smaller one and they found a "pretty Snug Cove." And this time Cook reports the matter that will rapidly change the complexion of affairs along the hitherto unregarded Northwest Coast. "A great many canoes filled with Natives were about the Ships all day, and a trade commenced betwixt us and them . . . Their articles were the skins of various animals such as Bears, Wolfs, Foxes, Dear, Rackoons, Polecats, Martins and *in particular the Sea Beaver* [author's italics], the same as found on the coast of Kamchatka." (Cook's *Journals*, March 30, 1778) Rion says April 1: "the sea beaver or Otter, the skin of which is very soft and delicate."

And thus was initiated a trade that would continue through 50 years, until the sea otter was almost extinct from Baja California up the long reaches arching over to the islands off Kamchatka and north of Japan.

Although Cook was at first but mildly satisfied with his anchorage, the ships remained there four weeks (See *Captain Cook's Approach to Oregon, 1778*, T. C. Elliott).

Among other things the very much decayed masts and rigging were gone over, another comment on the faulty yard work done before.

After further storms and gales and more repairs, Cook and Clerke moved up the coast and after a frustrating time in what is now Cook Inlet, moved through the Aleutians and north through the Bering Strait where in mid-August an impenetrable mass of ice was encountered at 70° 44′ north. It was similar to that met on the Second Voyage at 70° south, but with a more peaceful sea. Cook had in storm and night missed the Columbia River and Juan de Fuca Straits, but he noted the Kuskokwim and Yukon river flows as well as Bristol Bay. And after moving over to Cape Mys Shmidta above the Ichuktchis Peninsula of Siberia, it was moving pack ice that drove the ships down to Gulf of Anadyr. He parleyed with the savage Chukchis and then moved S.S.E. toward the Aleutians.

While aware of the historic anchorage at Petropavlovsk, Cook would also have been much aware of the physical and psychological damages of being trapped for months in Avatcha Bay. Too, he had seen no really hospitable place on the American coast since he missed the Puget Sound entrance. More certainly the Nootka Sound natives did not attract him or his crew, especially with Anderson gone. And everyone had fond memories of the Sandwich Islands, although no snug anchorage had been found.

After a cold and wet summer, the charms of the Islands easily lured them south. But they first refitted and repaired at Unalaska in what is now Dutch Harbor.

Charming as the islands are there are few safe anchorages even today, and Cook spent six weeks moving against contrary winds down and at last around the southern shore of the Big Island—Hawaii. At last they found a bay Bligh found reasonably safe and the ships entered in a state of exhaustion. It was called Kealakekua.

Although some distance from the northern islands, Cook was already well known here and over 1,000 canoes and swarms of swimmers and priests greeted him. Friendly trade ensued and a congenial contact was made especially with the monarch Terre'oboo (Kalaniopuu). They left on February 4, beating up the coast, but a small squall again damaged the rotten rigging. Very reluctantly Cook returned to the earlier anchorage where he was coolly received by the few natives remaining. They were alarmed by their increasing food shortage and the rather disappointing conduct of their blue eyed god. Store moving occurred along with increasing thievery of a serious nature. When the important cutter was stolen from *Discovery* by a minor chief, Cook decided to hold Terre'oboo hostage as he had other chiefs in similar situations. He went ashore with a few ill-trained marines and three boats. When the horde of natives became alarmed at the increasingly hostile atmosphere a melee exploded. Stones showered the sailors and restive marines. Shots were fired. Cook tried to signal in the general confusion. He fired a barrel of bird shot from his shot gun instead of a slug. The marines ran to the water and the enraged natives went after them beating the brains of four of them out upon the sharp coral.

For the moment Cook was no longer the god, Lono. Rather than falling on their faces the berserk natives shoved and clubbed and eventually stabbed him. A long dagger ironically made by one of the ship's armorers for trade purposes was driven into his neck. In his massive strength he kept moving through the bloody swirl, "not being able to swim he endeavoured to scramble on the Rock where a fellow gave him a blow on the head with a large Club and he was seen alive no more." (Samwell.) The shock was obvious on both sides. The crews "lost their father" and the natives a legendary god. The ships were actually fortunate to get away. In another atmosphere they might all have been overwhelmed.

Clerke took command and, sick as he was, again proceeded north to continue the island survey and then the northern passage search with Gore, now in command of *Discovery*. They arrived at Petropavlovsk, Kamchatka. They found it ice blocked. After communicating with the town and sending news of Cook's death overland toward Europe, the expedition moved again to beyond Bering Strait almost as deep into the ice as the preceding summer. But in every sense Cook's *Instructions* were filled to the letter. Beyond any doubt there was no Northwest Passage, at least not for the 18th century.

On August 22, Clerke died and was carried to Petropavlovsk for burial, and the great lieutenant to Cook rests there today beside astronomer la Croyère of Bering's expedition surrounded by a vast Russian Naval Base. Lieutenant Gore took command of the expedition with highly intelligent Lieutenant King as his second in *Discovery*.

After generous provisioning by the Russian garrison, 21 guns were fired to honor Catherine the Great and her solicitous Kamchatkan soldiers and natives. Off they moved into the Pacific, past the Japanese Islands and through the China and Java Seas, to Pulau Condore, the Strait of Banca and the Indian Ocean. What they left behind them in Canton was the momentous news of abundant sea otter herds on the Northwest Coast. Rudder problems obliged a stop at Capetown and then home. But as usual with the winds to which they were ever obligated, the tired ships moved up around the Orkneys and down through the North Sea toward Yarmouth, then the Thames and Deptford. This meant that Gore, the great hunter, returning safely home, took the straining crews past Whitby, the harbor mouth from which Cook had sailed as an apprentice 30 years earlier. Down the track where Cook had sailed carrying coal, Yarmouth to the Thames and Deptford. A voyage of four years and three months.

King George, who saw him but twice, knew Cook as monarch to subject and perhaps knew the magnificently resolute and supremely competent mariner in a manner others could not. The 40-year-old patriot King was much occupied with French threats and American wars, but it is said that George wept upon hearing the news of his great commander's death.

THE LEGACY OF CAPTAIN COOK

A. A. St. C. M. Murray-Oliver

What can one say of a man, unique in his own time, and timeless in his achievements? A man of humble birth, of little education, unknown at the age of 30—yet whose name is almost a household word throughout the civilized world two centuries later. A man who was afforded special protection by the Kings of France and Spain when his own country was locked in bitter warfare with theirs; and even by Benjamin Franklin, envoy to France from the then rebel American colonies struggling desperately to free themselves from hated British domination.

The latter half of the eighteenth century was the Age of Enlightenment, the Age of Science—and the Age of Privilege. How much the first two attributes outweighed the third may be seen by the tribute written by Admiral of the Fleet the Honorable John Forbes in the dedication to the official account of *Cook's Third Voyage*, published for the British Admiralty in 1784: "To the Memory of Captain James Cook, the ablest and most renowned Navigator this or any other country hath produced. He raised himself, solely by his merit, from a very obscure birth, to the rank of Post Captain in the Royal Navy . . . He possessed, in an eminent degree, all the qualifications requisite for his profession and great undertakings; together with the amiable and worthy qualities of the best men. . . . The death of this eminent and valuable man was a loss to mankind in general; and particularly to be deplored by every nation that respects useful accomplishments, that knows science, and loves the benevolent and amiable affections of the heart. It is still more to be deplored by this country, which may justly boast of having produced a man hitherto unequalled for nautical talents . . ."

Sir Francis Drake in the sixteenth century, Captain James Cook in the eighteenth, and Horatio, Viscount Nelson in the nineteenth—these are the three great names in British naval history. It is, however, only Cook whose accomplishments still benefit the world today, our own world. At this time of international tension, economic problems, social upheaval, many countries have united to pay tribute to James Cook in an unprecedented international exhibition held in that very country which broke away from his at the precise time that he was reaching the peak of his career.

Cook set out on his third great voyage of discovery and exploration one week after the American Declaration of Independence was signed in July, 1776. This was to be his last voyage. And he was to meet his death at the hands of the inhabitants of the last of his great discoveries—perhaps the greatest of them all—the Sandwich Islands, as he named the Hawaiian group. Here indeed was displayed the irony of fate; for it was thanks to Cook that the United States of America ultimately gained this rich addition to her territories.

When James Cook, unknown, newly-commissioned lieutenant, was sent to the South Seas in His Britannic Majesty's Bark *Endeavour* in 1768, nobody knew that, thanks to this one man, the next short decade would see the world enlarged more hugely and abruptly than in the thousand years preceding that date.

On his return from the First Voyage, Cook wrote to the Admiralty: "I flatter myself that the discoveries we have made, tho' not great, will apologize for the length of the voyage." And in return he was graciously informed that the Lords Commissioners of the Admiralty "extremely well approve of the whole of your proceedings." He was granted an hour-long audience with His Majesty King George the Third, who "was pleased to express his Approbation of my Conduct in Terms that were extremely pleasing to me," as Cook modestly mentioned in a letter to his old friend and former employer, John Walker, the shipowner of Whitby. It had been Walker who first taught his young sailor mathematics and navigation, thus making possible all that was to follow.

At the same audience at St. James Palace, Cook received his commission in the rank of Commander at the hands of the King himself. More pleasing than all these honors, however, to a man such as Cook, was the knowledge that, as he wrote even more modestly in that same letter: "I however have made no very great Discoveries yet I have exploar'd more of the Great South Sea than all that have gone before me so much that little remains now to be done to have a thorough knowledge of that part of the Globe."

Four years later Cook returned from his Second Voyage, "having been absent from England Three Years and Eighteen Days, in which time I lost but four men and only one of these by sickness." So wrote Cook succinctly but with justified pride. For on that voyage alone he had sailed more than 60,000 miles, an incredible achievement, an unparalleled triumph. Well might Cook write in the course of the Second Voyage, as he cruised the high latitudes of the Antarctic Ocean: "I whose ambition leads me not only further than any other man has been before me, but as far as I think it possible for man to go . . ." Even he did not realize just how far he had yet to go nor where his last most distant voyage would end.

Even a brief summary of his successive achievements is impressive in the great sweep of his varied activities. First, during the Seven Years' War between Great Britain and France, it was largely thanks to Cook's brilliant survey by and charting of the St. Lawrence River that General Wolfe was enabled to move up a great fleet of over 200 warships and transports to ensure the capture of Quebec from the French on 12 September 1759. Then, on the personal orders of Admiral Lord Colville, the Commander-in-Chief, Cook carried out a complete survey of the St. Lawrence from Montreal to the Atlantic, from which charts were made to replace those he rendered obsolete. So thorough was his work that many of his charts remained in use for more than a century.

Lord Colville awarded him the large sum of 50 guineas "in consideration of his indefatigable industry in making himself master of the pilotage of the River St. Lawrence." Later he informed the Admiralty "that from my experience of Mr. Cook's genius and capacity, I think him well qualified for the work he has performed and for greater undertakings of the same kind."

From 1762-67, James Cook continued survey work on the coast of Newfoundland and Labrador. These were of particular importance, not only to the Royal Navy but also to the economically very valuable cod-fishing industry. In 1766 he added new laurels to his already established reputation as an outstanding navigator and cartographer that was to be enhanced by each of his three great voyages. He now observed an eclipse of the sun and from his very accurate results calculated the correct longitude of Newfoundland. His report was published the following year in the *Philosophical Transactions* of the prestigious Royal Society, this in itself being no small honor. Moreover, the Society commented that the observer was "a good mathematician and very expert in his business."

Now came the First Voyage. At the age of 40 the man who had been a poor country boy of little education could look with pride upon a most praiseworthy career in the service of his King and country. Yet all this was only the prelude to his true career, which would make his name immortal in the realms of exploration. From the North Altantic that he knew so well Cook was about to be translated to the South Pacific, vast and virtually unknown. He conquered it, in those three tremendous voyages.

Cook might have been unknown to the public, to whom his choice to command *Endeavour* came as a surprise. But the Admiralty, and the Royal Society at whose request the First Voyage was authorized by the King, well knew the man they had chosen; they had solid grounds for satisfaction in their good fortune that such a man was available. His record to date was more than impressive to them.

The centuries-old myth of the existence of the Great South Land was almost demolished by Cook on the First Voyage alone. Further, although the Dutch explorer, Abel Janszoon Tasman, had first discovered the south coast of Australia and the west coast of New Zealand in 1642, he gave the world only the most sketchy outline of part of these two countries. He had made no attempt to chart the coasts accurately; he had carried out no exploration. Cook spent five months circumnavigating and charting the two main islands of New Zealand—surveying so accurately that some of these charts were not replaced until the time of his New Zealand Bicentenary in 1969. And he proved conclusively that New Zealand, at least, could not be part of the Great South Land, the fabled *Terra Australis Incognita,* as had been believed by many for over a century. He most literally put New Zealand on the map; thanks to Cook a new British nation was to arise, 12,000 miles away from England.

Cook had now carried out the mission he had been given. He could have returned home, but he was not that sort of man—rather, always he would "seek to strive, to find, and not to yield." He crossed the 1,200 miles of the stormy Tasman Sea to investigate New Holland, as Australia was then called. He discovered for the first time the great, fertile eastern seaboard, charted it and claimed it also for his King. Again, another new British nation was born, because of Cook.

The Second Voyage had necessarily to follow. The protagonists of the existence of a vast southern continent were still not wholly convinced. Cook and Banks had brought back from the First Voyage a vast deal of scientific information and thousands of drawings and specimens. Cook had made many accurate charts of the Society (Tahitian) Islands and New Zealand, and the most important part of Australia. But, possibly, it was said, there could yet be an unknown continent lying between New Zealand and South America. Cook was

convinced this was not so, but he was sent in 1775 to make certainty beyond dispute. He did so, once and for all.

More, he crossed the Antarctic Circle—first ever to do so—no less than five times, plunging deep into the treacherous iceberg-ridden Antarctic waters, further than any man before him, pushing almost to the Antarctic Continent itself, the existence of which was still unsuspected. But, in any case, that land was not the continent he sought. Northward to the tropics and a roll-call of "islands made solid," as Beaglehole superbly phrases it; for hitherto, though a new land might have been discovered, there was no guarantee it would ever be found again. The Tongan group—Cook's Friendly Islands—first found by Tasman in 1643; Easter Island, discovered in 1722 by the Dutchman Roggeveen; the Marquesas, discovered in 1595 by the Spaniard Mendara, but of notoriously uncertain position; the New Hebrides, first visited by another Spaniard, de Quiros, in 1606; and new discoveries, the Cook Islands, New Caledonia, and Norfolk Island.

And there was another new discovery, in another field. As he wrote: "It doth not become me to say how far the principal objects of our voyage have been obtained. Had we found out a continent there, we might have been better enabled to gratify curiosity; but we hope our not having found it, after all our persevering researches, will leave less room for future speculation about unknown worlds remaining to be explored. But whatever may be the public judgment about other matters, it is with real satisfaction, and without claiming any merit but of attention to my duty, that I can conclude this account with an observation which facts enable me to make, that our having discovered the possibility of preserving health amongst a numerous ship's company for such a length of time, in such varieties of climate, and amidst such continued hardships and fatigues, will make this voyage remarkable in the opinion of every benevolent person, when the disputes about a southern continent shall have ceased to engage the attention, and to divide the judgment of philosophers."

Until the First Voyage, the disease of scurvy had decimated the crews of ships engaged upon long voyages. There were many theories as to possible cures.

Cook himself made no great new discovery, but he did apply most meticulously the information available to him. And he conquered scurvy by obtaining fresh supplies especially of greens, at every possible opportunity; and by scrupulous attention to the hygiene of his men and his ships. On each voyage, Cook's measures proved successful.

The "philosophers" of the Royal Society—the leading scientific organization in the world—were certainly in no way divided upon the merits of what the practical man of the sea, with hard facts, had done toward preventing the death of seamen. On the First Voyage, until the unavoidable disaster of Batavia, Cook had not lost a single man from sickness. This defeat of the dread specter of scurvy would alone have made that voyage worthwhile, for it opened up new vistas for future explorations, hitherto impossible. After the Second Voyage Cook prepared two papers for the Royal Society, one concerning his experience of and theories on the tides of the Pacific, the other relating to his antiscorbutic practices. Both were published and received warm praise. On 29 February 1776, he was elected a Fellow of the Royal Society, a high honor in itself, to be numbered among the leading scientists and scholars of the kingdom.

Yet an even greater honor was also awarded him by the Royal Society. The Copley Gold Medal is the highest scientific honor the Society can bestow. In 1776 Cook was voted it by the Fellows for his contribution to the health of seamen, so important to a maritime nation, and this is the only time the medal has been awarded for advances in the study of nutrition. It was presented to Mrs. Cook by the President of the Society, Sir John Pringle, and she bequeathed it to the British Museum. At the time of the presentation Cook himself was well into the Third Voyage.

This voyage was inevitable. Cook had exhausted the possibilities of the South Seas. He had answered conclusively one great query—that of the existence of a southern continent. There was, however, a second enigma, the long sought Northwest Passage, linking the Atlantic and the Pacific oceans. If any man could find it, thought the Lords of the Admiralty, Cook could do so. He could not; he failed in this and he lost his own life, but he failed gloriously. And he discovered the Hawaiian Islands; he made many more charts, more particularly of the Northwest American coast, and Alaska, and the Aleutian Islands, and the Siberian shores, daring the perils of the Arctic just as he had those of the Antarctic.

More, again: when his ships sadly returned at long last to England, they brought with them splendid furs which spurred on the bold to open up the rich fur trading potential of the Pacific Northwest coast. So, as before, a new land was settled because of Cook.

Captain Cook died, and the whole world mourned, none more so than his own men. David Samwell wrote the most touching tribute: "He was beloved by his people, who looked up to him as to a father and obeyed his commands with alacrity. The confidence we placed in him was unremitting, our admiration of his great talents unbounded, our esteem for his good qualities affectionate and sincere. . . . In every situation he stood unrivalled and alone; on him all eyes were turned; he was our leading-star, which at its setting left us involved in darkness and despair."

James Cook had fired the imagination of all Europe, all the civilized world of his day. The accounts of his voyages were the best-sellers of that time and were quickly translated into French, German, Italian, and Russian. Condolences poured into London from all the crowned heads of Europe, led by Catherine the Great. The *London Gazette* of 8 February 1780 reported: "The Empress of Russia expressed a most deep Concern at the Loss of Captain Cook. She was the more sensibly affected from her very partial regard to his merits, and when she was informed of the Hospitality shewn by the Russian Government at Kamchatka to Captain Clerke, she said no subjects in her Dominions could show too much Friendship for the Survivors of Captain Cook."

The scientific results obtained on the three voyages aroused the greatest interest of scientists throughout the world. Much of what was recorded still provides an invaluable field for research. Objects collected on the voyages, pertaining to native cultures; manuscript accounts of the voyages; drawings and paintings made by artists on Cook's ships—all these were scattered into many countries over the years that followed. Until now most had never even been seen together. Only for this

Exhibition in Portland have so many of them been gathered together, 200 years later.

Explorer, navigator, cartographer, dietician, scientist —Cook was truly a man for all seasons. Even today our debt to him is immeasurable. Research will long continue into the rich legacy he bequeathed, not alone to his native Britain, nor to the many countries of British origin, but to all humanity.

The Royal Society, of which Cook's old companion Sir Joseph Banks was now President, unprecedentedly ordered a splendid gold medal to be struck in memory of Cook. In his letter to Mrs. Cook accompanying the medal, Banks wrote that it was "in consideration of the many services he did to the cause of science. As his friend, I join to yours my sincere regret for the loss this nation has suffered in the death of so valuable a man, and that which the Royal Society feels in so useful a member; but while we lament his loss with a tear of real affliction, we must not forget that his well-spent life secures to us who survive him, that best consolation, the recollection that his name will live forever in the remembrance of a people, grateful for the services his labours have afforded to mankind in general.

"Cease, then, Madame, to lament a man whose virtues have exacted a tribute of regret from a large portion of the natives of the earth . . ."

Not only a tribute of regret. Over 200 monuments to the memory of Cook now stand upon the face of the earth, many being in the countries that he himself first discovered.

It is recorded that King George the Third wept when he learned of the death of one of his most distinguished subjects. He granted a handsome pension to the explorer's widow. And he awarded Cook posthumously a coat-of-arms, the first step toward nobility. Its two mottoes could scarcely be more appropriate—*Circa orbem* (Around the Globe) and *Nil intentatum reliquit* (He left nothing unattempted).

I.

CAPTAIN JAMES COOK
By Sir Lionel Cust after John Webber. See Cat. no. 2.

1. CAPTAIN COOK'S CANNON

National Academy of Sciences, Philadelphia.

One of the harrowing experiences of the First Voyage was the entrapment in the atolls and reefs of the Great Barrier Reef on June 11, 1770. The *sang froid* of the Commander must have been sorely tried as the lonely *Endeavour* dragged from one sharp reef to another. Especially unbelievable is the fact that astronomer Charles Green, in a time most fraught with peril, with his assistants calmly noted lunar observations fixing the longitude from the deck of a ship that might sink at any moment.

Cook scarcely mentions the consternation that must have ranged through the overcrowded *Endeavour* when they crunched into the labyrinth of the Great Barrier Reef, but we know that every manner of stone and iron ballast, empty casks, condemned stores and other items were hurled overboard—almost 50 tons. At last they were reduced to the weight of the *Endeavour* armament, six cannons and their carriages, about 1,000 pounds each. They went over the side.

Cook may have vowed never again to sail one ship alone, for in that moment he was in the deepest trouble he ever encountered—and no assistance at hand.

About 200 years later, in 1969, an expedition returned to Pickersgill and Endeavor reefs. They found the guns, two of them still loaded with 4-pound balls. The wood carriages had disappeared and the iron was encased in four feet of living coral. Eventually all six cannons were restored.

We are most grateful to the Academy of Natural Sciences, Philadelphia, for generously loaning their 6-foot *Endeavour* cannon marked with the Royal Cypher "GR2". It was the Academy that financed the recovery expedition in 1968, and the Australian government kindly gave one of the restored cannons to the Academy and the United States.

2. CAPTAIN COOK (On the Third Voyage) After John Webber by Sir Lionel Cust. NPG, London.

The opinions of connoisseurs vary, of course. There are some who prefer the noble N. Dance portrait of Cook which hangs in Greenwich. It is in every sense official—reserved and yet attractive in its severity. After all, Cook had just returned from the greatest voyage of all time—his Second Voyage being the equivalent of more than a journey around Earth at its equatorial circumference.

But others prefer Webber's curiously hard yet jaunty three-quarter portrait—a twist of the conventional and highly individual—which makes one think a better likeness was caught. This portrait by Sir Lionel Cust was taken from the splendid Webber proudly hanging in the National Art Gallery, Wellington. It seems to epitomize the Captain Cook of history,

even though Mrs. Cook thought it "too severe."

3. CAPTAIN HUGH PALLISER (1723-96)

Oil painting by Sir Nathaniel Dance, M.P., R.A. (1735-1811). Loan Marion Davies Collection, Los Angeles County Museum of Art, an oil painting attributed to George Dance (1741-1825) after portrait by Sir Nathaniel Dance. NMG, London.

This is an unusual exhibition situation in which we have the original oil of Captain Hugh Palliser (1723-96) by Sir Nathaniel Dance of the brilliant George Dance (1700-68) family and a copy attributed to George Dance, Jr., Nathaniel's younger brother. The portrait on the left was copied from the conventional yet elegant original for presentation to Greenwich Hospital by Sir Hugh Palliser, the 3rd baronet, in 1825. Like Cook, Palliser is seen here as a senior Captain (1767-74), and looking much as Cook would have known him. Palliser was also a Yorkshireman and it was he who served as Captain of the *Eagle* (60 guns) when Cook served as Able Seaman (AB), Master's Mate, and Boatswain. Palliser had come up from First Lieutenant in the *Essex* where he had seen bloody service, including the Battle of Toulon. Palliser went on to become Commodore and Governor of Newfoundland and again noticed Cook, who had risen to Master and acquired his notable surveying skills. Palliser was responsible for Cook's assignment to command the survey ship *Grenville*.

Palliser's career was in several ways troubled and indecisive, although he became a Governor at Greenwich Hospital (a sinecure) and an Admiral of the White. Perhaps his claim to fame was his unswerving support of Cook including support of his appointment to command *Grenville* and his subsequent promotion to officer status as Lieutenant.

4. PORTRAIT (ca 1770) OF SIR HUGH PALLISER (1723-96)

By Sir Nathaniel Dance-Holland, Bart. M.P., R.A. 124.5 x 101.7 cm. Oil painting on canvas. LACMA, Los Angeles, from the Marion Davies collection.

Compare this with a version also exhibited, copied by George Dance (1741-1825) from this original in 1825 for presentation to the Greenwich Hospital by Sir Hugh Palliser, the 3rd baronet. Now in NMG, London. Nathaniel Dance made the most popular painting of Cook (now at Greenwich) in 1776. He studied art in London and Italy and was a foundation member of the Royal Academy, exhibiting portraits of George III and Queen Charlotte. He was created a baronet in 1800. In his day Dance was the most fashionable portraitist in London, hence Banks chose him to paint Cook's portrait. When Dance entered Parliament he gave up painting for a political career no one remembers.

7.

IO

8.

5. JOHN, 4TH EARL OF SANDWICH (*1718-92*)
Oil painting by Thomas Gainsborough, R.A. (1727-88).
108" x 72". NMG, London.

The 4th Earl was painted by Gainsborough in 1783, with the dome of Greenwich Hospital appropriately looming behind him. A man of obvious energies, Sandwich had served in top posts of the Admiralty, first in 1744 when he became a Commissioner and as First Lord in 1748. He had worked with Anson in correction and reform of the royal dockyards. Dismissed in 1751 the licentious reformer was returned for two years in 1763 when Cook was charting the Newfoundland coast.

In 1771 he was returned for his third term of office, where he served during the American Revolution and Cook's last two voyages. He was with Palliser a principal patron of the great navigator. Though his fleets lost strategic command in the Atlantic at a most critical juncture of the War for Independence, here he stands aloof in lordly confidence. The war was lost, but at the close of his 12-year reign he is the acknowledged strategist of two Pacific voyages by his protege that will live forever in memory, and a legendary archipelago sometimes bears his name.

6. WEDGWOOD PLAQUE BEARING PORTRAIT OF COOK
Executed by John Flaxman after the likeness by William Hodges, R.A. ATL, Wellington, N.Z.

The more usual smaller Wedgwood medallion of Cook by Flaxman, derived from the Dance portrait, is reproduced on the cover of the Hakluyt Society's edition of Cook's *Journals*, edited by J. C. Beaglehole. This larger representation, believed to be an unique example, was purchased by the late Mr. Turnbull with much jubilation, despite the fact that it was already cracked. He treasured it so greatly that this was the sole item he bequeathed to his younger sister, Joanna, Lady Leigh-Wood, of London. When Sir James and Lady Leigh-Wood visited the Alexander Turnbull Library in the late 1940s, she presented it to the Library, thinking that her brother would have liked it to become once more part of his Cook collection.

7. CHRISTOPHER COLUMBUS, *Discoverer* (*1446-1506*)
13¾" x 16½". NMG, London.
Christopher Columbus whose likeness is reflected in this approximation engraved by Stradanus (born 17 years after the death of the Admiral of the Ocean Sea) is known as one of the greatest explorers of all time. He first crossed the North Atlantic from east to west in 1492. As the discoverer of the New World he will be forever remembered. Columbus, too, made three voyages and achieved renown almost 300 years before

Cook. In any comparison Columbus must rank perhaps with Magellan, Vasco da Gama and Bering, just below Cook.

8. FERDINAND MAGELLAN, *Navigator* (*ca 1470-1521*)
Copperplate engraving by Stradanus, 14¼" x 16¼".
NMG, London.

He first discovered a strait below the Americas leading from the Atlantic to the Pacific Ocean in the *Victoria*. Reaching the Philippine Islands in 1520, he was there killed by natives in an intertribal war in which he had unwisely intruded. Of the five vessels in the expedition the *Victoria* alone returned to Spain.

The renowned pilot is shown here making use of the new art of nautical astronomy developed by the Portuguese in the 15th century to make oceanic navigation possible. He is measuring on an armillary sphere with a pair of dividers.

9. NAUTICAL ASTRONOMY IN THE 16TH CENTURY
Copperplate engraving by Stradanus (1523-d ca 1605),
14" x 16¼". NMG, London.

A navigator is shown taking an observation with an instrument especially designed to determine the magnetic variation affecting the ship's compass. This knowledge was used to find true courses and bearings, and magnetic variation was also used in an attempt to determine a ship's longitude at sea.

The Latin text reads in translation: "the world's longitude discovered from the magnet's declination from the Pole. Plancius enables one to find one's port everywhere by means of the magnet which often declines a little on one side or the other."

Peter Plancius (1552-d 1622) was a Dutch cosmographer who devoted much effort to collecting measurements of variation and urging their publication for the use of longitude determination at sea. Courtesy NMG.

10. SIR FRANCIS DRAKE, CIRCUMNAVIGATOR (*ca 1540-96*)
Line engraving by W. Marshall, 1648. 10" x 8½".
NMG, London.

Naturally there is much interest in this fierce and redoubtable Englishman, the first to sail around the world (1577-80) in the renowned *Golden Hind*. The precise location of his California anchorage in "New Albion" may be uncertain, but we are convinced that he first saw the Oregon coast off the dunes at Florence or Coos Bay, causing him to remark on snow covered mountains as well as the oft mentioned "vile, stinking fogge."

So Cook 200 years later described his Oregon landfalls almost at the point where Drake turned again to the south. The capes Cook saw we still know today as Perpetua and Foulweather. We might assume that Cook, too, might have been knighted upon his third voyage home, as Gloriana

11.

15.

13.

knighted "Red Beard" amidst cheering Plymouth crowds. Elizabeth smiled upon Drake and George III wept on the news of Cook's death.

11. COMMODORE GEORGE ANSON, CIRCUMNAVIGATOR (1697-1762)
Line engraving by C. Grignion after A. Pond, 1774. 12″ x 8½″. NMG, London.

Anson's celebrated voyage of circumnavigation in 1740 was successful, excepting the horrendous loss of life from scurvy. Especially since two years after his departure, Anson in the *Centurion* captured the annual Manila treasure galleon. England was more or less at war with Spain during this period, ostensibly because of Jenkins' Ear, and discipline was taut. But the facts of the superb Anson voyage underline the later and greater achievement by Cook. Of the 961 who left England in Anson's three-ship squadron 626 died, mainly from scurvy. The ships were overloaded with crew members to make up for the not unexpected losses. Until Cook's time this was almost routine procedure. When Cook began his survey as Master's Mate in Newfoundland, Anson was a venerable Admiral of the Fleet. He died in 1762.

12. CHART OF THE KNOWN WORLD, 1755
By Sr. Jacques Bellin, Département de la Marine et du Depôt des Plans, France. 38″ x 26¾″. Loan NMG. See front endsheet.

Being a French chart, the Prime Meridian runs through the Paris Observatory, but a traditional longitude scale based on the Island of Ferro in the Canary Islands is also included. It is drawn on Mercator's projection.

Note, south of Africa, Cap de la Circoncision sighted in fog by Lozier Bouvet on New Year's Day, 1739, and believed by him to be a point of the Great Southern Continent.

Eastern Australia is unknown, Tasmania only partially charted, New Zealand even less so.

The rest of the South Pacific is conveniently covered by cartouches. In the North Pacific the coastline of America is unknown north of San Francisco: "*tout ceci est inconnu*"—all here is unknown.

Unfortunately Bellin's brilliant surmises led to many mistakes entered in *L'Hydrographic Francoise* (1756) including the elusive Solomons discussed by Helen Wallis in *Carteret* (1963).

13. CAPTAIN THE HON. JOHN BYRON (1723-86)
Oil painting by Sir Joshua Reynolds, R.A. (1723-92), 30″ x 25″. NMG, London.

Byron had sailed as a midshipman with Lord Anson in HMS *Wager* (24), during the celebrated circumnavigation (1740-44). *Wager* was lost to the squadron when she wrecked on the coast of Chile.

In June, 1764 "Capt.Jack" Byron was in command of the copper-sheathed frigate *Dolphin*, attended by the sloop *Tamar*. He sighted the Falkland Islands in the South Atlantic which he dubbed Pepys' Island. Passing through the Straits of Magellan he found his ships too much damaged to sail toward the California coast and the elusive Northwest Passage. He continued across the South Pacific down through the Indian Ocean to the Cape of Good Hope. He returned his scurvy-ravaged crews to England in May, 1766.

Ten years later Byron was Commander-in-Chief of the North American Station. There he fought and lost the strategically important engagement off Grenada against the French fleet under d'Estaing. "Mad Jack" outlived Cook, dying in 1786 as a Vice-Admiral of the White.

He was painted by England's "greatest portraitist" midway in their careers.

14. BYRON'S JOURNAL, 1764-66
This journal, although apparently a copy, is unique and is one of the few accounts of the voyage known. NMG, London.

As soon as the Seven Years War (1756-63) was ended, Britain renewed the interest in the Pacific which Anson's voyage 20 years before had done so much to arouse. With the lively support of the young king, George III, Captain the Hon. John Byron, with *Dolphin* and *Tamar*, was dispatched to gain control of the eastern approaches to the Pacific by annexing the Falkland Islands, lying off the southern approach, and to search for a northern passage between the Pacific and Atlantic oceans. However, finding his ships unseaworthy for this northern venture, Byron crossed the Pacific in the tropics and returned home. Courtesy NMG.

15. LOUIS-ANTOINE, CHEVALIER DE BOUGAINVILLE, *Explorer (1729-1811)*
Stipple engraving by Wachsman Awton, 12″ x 8″. NMG.

During the Seven Years War (1756-63), de Bougainville was aide-de-camp to the chivalrous Marquis de Montcalm in Canada where Cook was working for Wolfe on the St. Lawrence Channel. With the coming of peace, de Bougainville transferred from the French army to the navy. He offered to found a French settlement in the Falkland Islands at his own expense. When Byron annexed the islands in the name of George III in 1765, a French colony had been established there a year.

Spain had earlier claimed the islands and, in November, 1755, de Bougainville sailed in *La Bourdeuse* to return the islands to France's Spanish ally, and to cross the Pacific to the East Indies. He carried on board a naturalist, Philibert de Commerson, and a young astronomer, Verron, who was eager

16.

Alex. Dalrymple.

17.

to try methods of finding longitude at sea, particularly the method of lunar distances developed by the astronomer Lacaille, using an English reflecting quadrant. At times he and Cook were less than 100 miles from each other.

De Bougainville reached Tahiti in April, 1768, and St. Malo in March, 1769. The attractive Chevalier is well remembered but his credits as a major explorer are thin.

16. PORTRAIT OF ALEXANDER DALRYMPLE
Engraving by George Dance, 1794. 8″ x 10½″.
ATL, Wellington, N.Z.

Dalrymple was born under the wrong star. He was obviously mentally energetic and possessed of some ideas, but he seems to have been born under a crossed star where Cook was showered by a field. Captain Dalrymple had some exceptional sea and hydrographic experience, but at the risk of seeming brash one might suggest that the 18th was not his century, nor would any have been thereafter.

He seemed forever assigned to pose problems which Cook or a colleague would unravel and solve. And yet for this very reason we should perhaps realize our debt to Captain Dalrymple. He proposed the Transit of Venus expedition.

17. CAPTAIN SAMUEL WALLIS ATTACKED IN MATAVAI BAY, TAHITI, *1767*
A representation of the attack on Captain Wallis in Dolphin *by the natives of Otaheite. 17½″ x 20¾″. Engraving by E. Rooker. NMG, London.*

After the island had been annexed by hoisting a pennant and turning a sod, the last sign of enmity was a mass demonstration three days later, dispersed by shooting of the ship's guns. The next day the natives were convinced that the ship wished merely to trade for provision—hogs, fruits and fowls were then quickly provided. The sick, the results of scurvy, were then taken on shore. The description of this voyage along with those of Commodore John Byron and Wallis' associate, Carteret, not to mention Cook's First Voyage, were all given in a rich commission to Dr. John Hawkesworth. He experienced a miserable editorial failure and died from worry and fret in 1773.

18. TAHITI SURRENDERED TO CAPTAIN WALLIS, *1767*
A representation of the surrender of the island of Otaheite to Captain Wallis by the supposed Queen Oberea. Engraving by J. Hall. 17¼″ x 20¼″. NMG, London.

Captain Wallis, during his voyage around the world in search of the "Great Southern Continent," first sighted Otaheite (or Tahiti) on 18 June 1767. He named it King George the Third's Island. At that moment of sunset, some of his men thought they saw, farther to the south still, the outline of a continental coast. This was believed to be part of the supposed Great Southern Continent.

When Wallis returned to England, Tahiti was selected as the point of observation in the Pacific of the Transit of Venus of 1769. This choice was possible as Wallis's purser, Harrison, had observed the longitude, using lunar distances, as well as the latitude, so that the island's exact geographical position was known. Courtesy NMG.

From J. Hawkesworth, *An Account of the Voyages undertaken . . . for Making Discoveries in the Southern Hemisphere,* London (1773), Vol. 1, Pl. 22.

19. THE SEAMAN'S DAILY ASSISTANT, *1763*
Thomas Haselden. NMG, London.

This was one of the books provided by the Board of Longitude for Cook's officers, largely because of the astronomical and geometrical tables it contained.

20. HOLOGRAPH LETTERS AND DOCUMENTS OF AND RELATIVE TO CAPTAIN JAMES COOK. *1764*
ATL, Wellington, N.Z.

Contains letters from Cook to the Admiralty while serving his first command in schooner *Grenville* while surveying the coast of Newfoundland. The volume contains his journal and drawings of elevations as well as letters.

21. THREE TRANSCRIPTS OF LETTERS TO JAMES COOK, MASTER OF THE SURVEY SCHOONER *GRENVILLE,* AT DEPTFORD, *1765*
APL, Auckland, N.Z.

17 January 1765, in an unknown hand; from the Victualling Office, London, to Cook as Commander of the *Grenville,* relating to the victualling of the vessel for a voyage to Newfoundland.

24 February 1765, transcript in Cook's hand; from the Navy Office, London, informing him that he is being supplied with the colors demanded by him.

10 April 1765, in an unknown hand; from the Victualling Office, London, informing him that the provisions and beer requested by him will be sent to the *Grenville.* In this first command Cook achieved solid reputation as a master hydrographer, surveyor, and scientific observer. During this voyage he prepared his paper on the eclipse of the sun, which was so well received by the Royal Geographical Society.

22. COOK TO VICTUALLING OFFICE
Original letter of July 13, 1768. NLA, Canberra, Australia.

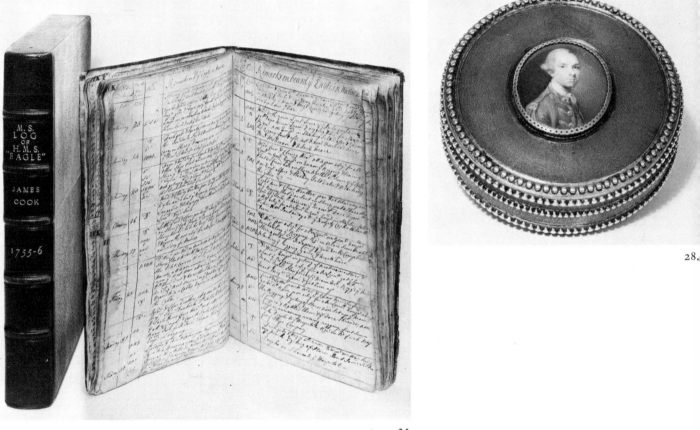

25.

28.

23. HOLY BIBLE CONTAINING THE OLD AND NEW TESTAMENTS (*Oxford: M. Baskett, 1765.*)
ML, LNSW, Sydney, Australia.

Bears the bookplate—possibly posthumous—of Captain Cook. On the authority of Mrs. Cook, this Bible is said to have been used by him in conducting Divine Service; manuscript letter tipped in.

Although Zimmerman in his *Account of the Third Voyage* makes a point of writing: "He never mentioned religion, and would have no priests on his ships; and, although he seldom celebrated the Sabbath, he was a just and upright man in all his dealings," in fact Cook took a service himself for the whole crew every Sunday morning and read the lessons from this Bible. It was returned to his widow, who cherished and used it for the rest of her very long life.

24. ORIGINAL MANUSCRIPT ACCOUNT OF WORK ON A SHIP'S DAY, ON HMS *EAGLE*, *3 November 1756*
By James Cook, Master's Mate. ML, LNSW, Sydney, Australia.

Transferred to the Mitchell Library from the Australian Museum, October, 1955.

Compare this with Cook's log kept on *Eagle* at this time, also in the exhibition.

25. LOG OF HMS *EAGLE* (*1755-56*)
James Cook, Original, ATL, Wellington, New Zealand.

Cook's career in HMS *Eagle* (60) was not without crisis. Aside from the daily aspect of living in a crowded warship on patrol and blockade, there are the plain facts of shattering engagements at sea in the 17th and 18th centuries. "Hearts of Oak" the men may have been, but the decks and hulls were also solid oak which tore into razored splinters, flying in a thousand shards with heavy cannonade. And Cook had his share in *Eagle* as Master's Mate, especially against the *Duc d'Aquitaine* when 80 were wounded. He was lucky to survive the flying balls and bar iron when *Eagle's* "mast and rigging were very much shattered."

But here we see him in his more routine moments and under the eye of the new Captain, Hugh Palliser, a fellow Yorkshireman who would become his constant but demanding patron.

26. CHART MADE BY COOK OF ST. LAWRENCE RIVER BELOW QUEBEC
Facsimile copy. Courtesy, BM.

This is a superb visual proof of Cook's months of expert tutelage from Samuel Holland, working in the St. Lawrence estuary. Working from HMS *Pembroke* with the encouragement of Captain John Simcoe, Cook became not only an able shipmaster but also a master surveyor. Cook and his associates resurveyed the tricky St. Lawrence channel through rapids from which French military engineers had removed the markers.

Eventually Wolfe's troops ascended the water passage to a point where they could reach the Plains of Abraham, where General Wolfe was killed. Holland later became Surveyor General of Quebec.

27. ELIZABETH COOK'S FURNITURE
NMG, London.

This furniture belonged to the widow of Captain James Cook who lived for 56 years after her husband's death. She died in 1835, being 93 years old, and was buried in Cambridge. *Mahogany tray.*

This is fitted with inserts to hold a service of china or plate, presumably for safety, for it may have been used at sea by Captain Cook.
Mahogany chest of drawers with original pulls.

A slide pulls forward from beneath the top. Courtesy NMG.

28. SILVER SNUFFBOX BELONGING TO ADMIRAL ISAAC SMITH, R.N. (*1752-1831*)
NLA, Canberra, Australia.

Isaac Smith, one of the longest-lived of the explorers, was a cousin of Mrs. Cook. He had served with Cook in *Grenville* as an A.B. and joined *Endeavour* in the same capacity, becoming Master's Mate in 1771. Cook allowed him the honor of being the first European to set foot on the eastern coast of Australia, at Botany Bay, New South Wales, 29 March 1770. Beaglehole records that both Mrs. Cook and the Admiral frequently recounted that Cook, on the point of stepping ashore, said to the youth: "Isaac, you shall land first," and he followed. Cook found him "very expert" in surveying. On the Second Voyage Smith was Master's Mate in *Resolution*. He achieved the rank of Post Captain in 1787. In 1789 he served under Lord Cornwallis on the East India Station. In 1804 he was retired with the rank of Rear-Admiral. For many years before his death Admiral Smith kept Mrs. Cook company, the cousins living at his house at Merton Abbey, Surrey, in the summer and at her house in Clapham in the winter.

Cook praised Isaac Smith as being "clever and steady." His log for the First and Second Voyages is held in the Public Record Office, London. In the Mitchell Library, Sydney, are two letters from Smith, one dated 8 October 1830, stating that Mrs. Cook no longer had in her possession any papers in the Captain's hand, and that she felt hurt by the idea that Cook was ever considered severe; she had always found fault with Webber's portrait of him (now in the National Art Gallery, Wellington, N.Z.) for its stern look. The writer, sailing with him, had never thought him severe; Cook was loved and properly feared by his crews.

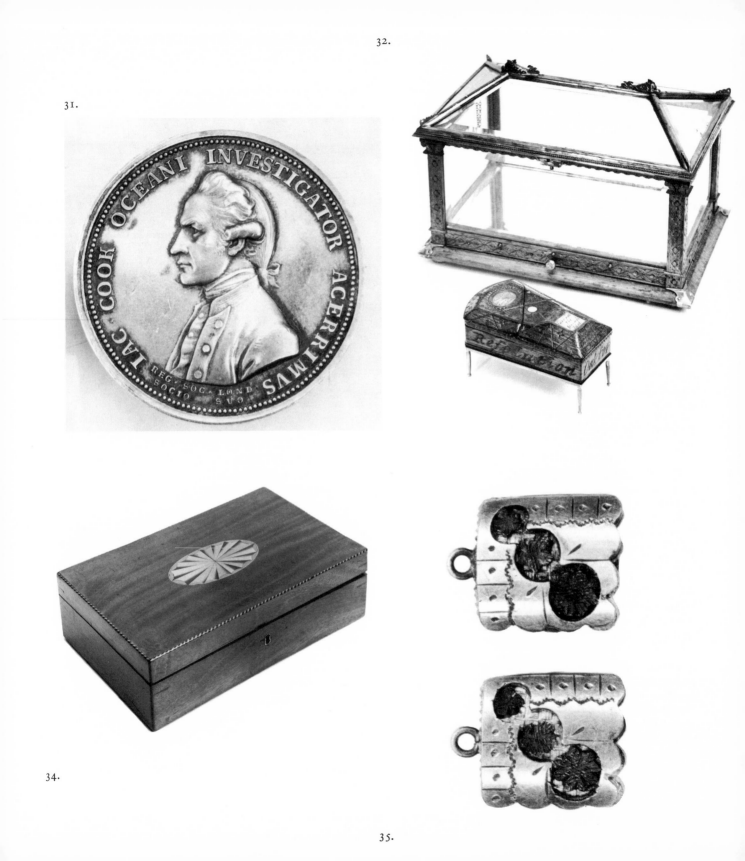

31.

32.

34.

35.

Along with this presentation snuff box the Mitchell Library also holds several original drawings by Smith, some being in an album of 97 original sketches, drawings, maps, etc., collected by him on the First and Second Voyages. This was acquired by the Government of New South Wales from the Admiral's relative, Cannon Bennett, also a close friend of Mrs. Cook. The album includes a number of excellent paintings by William Hodges and Henry Roberts.

29. LARGE KNIFE AND FORK, AND SMALL KNIFE, ALL WITH WOODEN HANDLES AND SILVER BANDS AT EACH END, USED BY COOK. (*From a set of 6 knives and 6 forks.*)
SILVER TABLE SPOON, GRAVY SPOON, AND CABIN SPOON, *all engraved with the crest of Captain Cook.*
ML, LNSW, Sydney, Australia.

These, if used by Cook, must have had the crests engraved upon them by Mrs. Cook for her own use, since his coat-of-arms was bestowed by King George III after Cook's death.

The tablespoon is one of a set of six and the cabin spoon one of a set of 12; all the above were transferred to the Mitchell Library from the Australian Museum, October, 1955.

30. STEEL, SILVER AND WOOD FORK BELONGING TO CAPTAIN COOK
NLA, Canberra, Australia.

31. TWO SILVER MEDALS
ATL, Wellington, N.Z.

With the approval of the Lords of the Admiralty, Cook arranged for the striking of medals in silver, copper, and brass to be taken on the Second Voyage and "to be given to the natives of new discovered countries and left there as testimonies of our being the first discoverers." They bore, on the obverse, the portrait of King George III and on the reverse the two ships of the expedition, *Resolution* and *Adventure*. Cook distributed these medals at three places in New Zealand—Dusky Sound, Queen Charlotte Sound, and off the entrance to Wellington harbor. Only six have been recovered in New Zealand and four on various Pacific islands.

After Cook's death the Royal Society had a medal struck in his honor, in 1784. Sir Joseph Banks, as President of the Society, proposed this commemoration, and it was designed by Lewis Pingo, engraver to the Royal Mint, where it was struck in gold, silver, and bronze. Banks transmitted one of the gold medals to Mrs. Cook with a sincere if fulsome tribute; she bequeathed it to the British Museum together with Cook's Copley Medal.

Banks wrote to the widow, from Soho Square, London, on

12 August 1786 that the Cook Medal was "in consideration of the many services he did to the cause of science. As his friend, I join to yours my sincere regret for the loss this nation has suffered in the death of so valuable a man . . ."

Both medals were bequeathed to the Turnbull Collections in 1961 by William Dubois Ferguson, Esq. of Wellington.

32. CARVED, COFFIN SHAPED DITTY BOX, ON SILVER STAND, CONTAINING A ROUGH WATER-COLOR SKETCH OF THE DEATH OF COOK, WITH A LOCK OF HIS HAIR AND DOCUMENT OF IDENTIFICATION: *and inscribed: made of RESOLUTION oak for Mrs. Cook by crew*
9 x 6.5 cm., enclosed in silver-mounted glass box measuring 16.6 x 23 x 15 cm. ML, LNSW, Sydney, Australia.

Inset in the lid are two silver plates inscribed "Quebec, Newfoundland, Greenwich, Australia" and "Lono and the Seaman's Idol." Inset in the bottom is a third silver plate inscribed "Captain James Cook Slain at Owhyee, 14 February, 1779."

A sliding compartment in the bottom of the case contains a description by Thomas Hart of how the box was made, and a Statutory Declaration signed by C. Albert Maggs dated 19.8.12 stating that Thomas Hart was a relative of Mrs. Cook, but he does not appear as a crew member on the Third Voyage.

33. TWO-FOOT IVORY RULE, MOUNTED WITH SILVER, WITH COOK'S CIPHER
ML, LNSW, Sydney, Australia.

34. INLAID WOOD DRESSING CASE USED BY COOK,
Inlay similar to that in cabin tea-caddy used on board RESOLUTION. ML, LNSW, Sydney, Australia.

Both pieces were transferred to the Library from the Australian Museum in October, 1955; correspondence accompanying the rule gave its source as J. Mackrell, one of Mrs. Cook's closest friends, whose memories of her provide almost the only description we have of Cook's widow.

35. CAPTAIN COOK'S CUFFLINKS
OHS Collections, 1957.

A pair of filled gold cufflinks in the collection of the Oregon Historical Society: reputed to have been presented by Mrs. James Cook to her husband's elder brother who was the great-uncle of Mary Offutt McBride, grandmother of the donor, Mrs. Albert Powers, Oregon City.

36. CHART OF COOK'S VOYAGES AND DISCOVERIES, *1768-80*

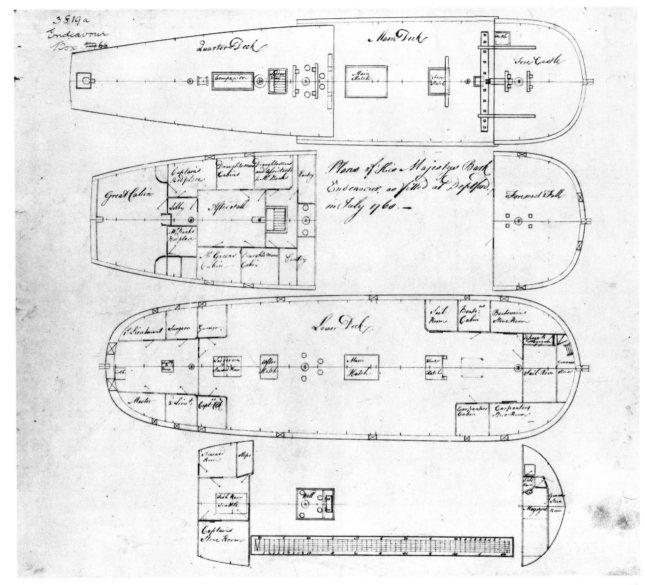

Plans of His Majestys Bark
Endeavour, as fitted at Deptford,
in July 1768 —

38.

Near the end of his Second Voyage, Cook had summed up his achievements in the South Pacific. On his return, he had been appointed to a lucrative and leisured post at Greenwich Hospital where Palliser held a preferment. The Admiralty had plans now to have done in the North Pacific what Cook had done in the South. But, his first biographer recounts: "The benefits he had already conferred on science and navigation, and the labors and dangers he had gone through, were so many and so great, that it was not deemed reasonable to ask him to engage in fresh perils . . . However Captain Cook was so fired with the contemplation and representation of the object, that he started up, and declared he himself would undertake the direction of the enterprise . . ."

"Captain Cook was appointed to the command of the expedition on the 10th of February, 1776." A. Kippis, *The Life of Captain James Cook* (London, 1788), pp. 324-25.

Dr. Kippis knew personally Sandwich, the First Lord of the Admiralty; Sir Hugh Palliser on the Board, and Mr. Philip Stephens, the Secretary. They all dined at Lord Sandwich's with Cook to discuss the projected North Pacific voyage to find the long sought Northwest Passage. They thus lured him, "the willing prisoner," through his continuing intellectual curiosity, into taking a command before he was rested from his previous voyages. The strain began to show early in the Third Voyage as his *visage de fer* slowly eroded—from the inside.

37. PART OF THE *ENDEAVOUR'S* STERNPOST
NMG, London.

After her return to England in 1771, *Endeavour* was sent out to the Falkland Islands as a store ship. She was therefore not available for Cook's Second Voyage.

Endeavour was sold out of the Service in 1775, and reverted to her original role of North Sea collier.

In 1790 *Endeavour* was purchased from a firm in Dunkirk and consigned to Newport, R.I. under French colors, as *La Liberte*; there she later ran aground and was abandoned. Some of these well-authenticated relics were preserved in the neighborhood of Newport whence this one—a generous gift—came to NMG from the Newport Historical Association, 1968.

38. *ENDEAVOUR* DECK PLANS, *1768*
NMG, London.

On 21 March, 1768, the Navy Board recommended to the Lords Commissioners of the Admiralty to "make choice of a cat-built vessel" for the voyage to the Pacific "which in their kind are roomly and will afford the advantage of stowing and carrying a large quantity of provisions so necessary on such voyages."

Of three such vessels then in the Thames, the officers at Deptford Yard reported most favorably on *The Earl of Pembroke*, Whitby built, 106 feet long overall, her extreme breadth 29 feet 3 inches, her tonnage 368. With a wide bluff bow— that is, cat-built—she could run at seven or eight knots, and was a typical east coast collier.

By early April she was being "sheathed and filled"—being given a further skin, outside her planks, of thinner boards and, to give protection against the worm, the destructive *Teredo navalis* of tropical seas, the sheathing was filled with nails with large flat heads. (Wallis's *Dolphin* had been sheathed experimentally with copper—the final solution—but its repair far from base presented problems, as did the corrosion of ironwork resulting from its use.) Between 5 and 12 April Mr. James Cook was appointed to command the *Endeavour* and, on 21 July, sailed in her from Deptford.

On 22 July Cook was directed to receive on board not only Mr. Green, the assistant astronomer from Greenwich Observatory and his servant, but also Joseph Banks, Esq., F.R.S., and his suite of eight persons.

At Plymouth, therefore, reached on the 31st, "several shipwrights and Joiners from the Yard (were) Employ'd on board refitting the Gentlemens Cabbins and making a Platform over the Tiller . . ." One might imagine Cook's private thoughts. Courtesy NMG.

(J. C. Beaglehole, *The Journals of Captain James Cook*, Cambridge, 1955, Vol. 1, p. 2.)

39. DOCUMENTS RELATING TO CAPTAIN COOK
Original manuscripts entitled "Miscellaneous Material, 1768-84." ATL, Wellington, N.Z.

This volume contains five letters as well as a fragment of an unidentified journal from the *Endeavour* voyage, May 27-August 20, 1768 and June 24-29, 1769; part of a vocabulary of the language of the natives of Tanna in the New Hebrides. Here is another example of Cook's incredible contributions to the birth of ethnography as well as linguistics. The contributions of his gifted observers and recorders in these fields have been inadequately appraised.

40. CAPTAIN COOK'S JOURNAL OF HIS FIRST VOYAGE ROUND THE WORLD, *1893*
Limited edition, bound in wood from Cook's Elm Tree, Clapham Common. ATL, Wellington, N.Z.

Introduction by Captain Wharton, R.N. It was Wharton who said of Cook's stormy Van Diemen landfall: "The

43.

4·

mingled audacity and caution of Cook's navigation off this coast must awake the admiration of every seaman.''

41. LOG OF *ENDEAVOUR* BY FIRST OFFICER ZACHARY HICKS
ATL, Wellington, N.Z.

Lieutenant Hicks was a fine seaman who had come up from the lower decks as had Cook. He was a London born man who was, at 29, serving as an acting lieutenant on a sloop of war before being transferred as second in command to Cook on *Endeavour*, May, 1768.

One judges that he had all the great attributes of a second man with a fatal flaw—he boarded the ship with tuberculosis which eventually killed him: ''. . . it may be truly said that he hath been dieing ever sence, tho he held out tollerable untill he got to Batavia.'' Cook admired him.

42. LIEUTENANT PHILIP CARTERET'S HADLEY QUADRANT, *1761*
Inscribed: Lieut. Philip Carteret 1761; Cole Maker Fleet Street, London. 16" x 19". NMG, London.

Carteret, in command of the singularly misnamed *Swallow*, sloop, sailed from Plymouth under Captain Wallis in *Dolphin* with a store ship on 22 August 1766, to discover the supposed Southern Continent. They reached the Straits of Magellan on 17 December to emerge some four storm-battered months later into the Pacific, where the ships parted.

So parlous was the *Swallow's* state that Carteret decided he would have to return home at once by crossing the Pacific in the tropics. He did so, discovering Pitcairn Island and reaching Spithead on 20 May 1769, exactly a year *after* Wallis had reached Downs.

The Hadley Reflecting Quadrant

Hadley's invention of the reflecting quadrant, which he described to the Royal Society in 1731, was an essential invention in the process of developing practicable methods of determining a ship's longitude at sea. It enabled observations of the altitude of the sun and stars to be taken with sufficient accuracy to determine the ship's local time as well as her latitude. Developed in the 1750s into the sextant, it enabled observations of the angular distance between the sun and moon, or moon and a zodiacal star, to be taken with sufficient accuracy to determine the ship's longitude to within, on average, 30 miles—a quite unprecedented degree of accuracy.

The radius of this instrument is $17\frac{3}{8}$ inches, the frame of mahogany and the index arm and mirror mounts of brass. The vernier index reads to one minute of arc. The peepsights and glass shades are missing. Courtesy NMG.

43. 18-INCH HADLEY'S SEXTANT, *about 1770*
Inscribed: J. Bird, London. 22" x 31". NMG.

Used for measuring angles ashore and afloat.

The two main sources of error in early Hadley's quadrants and sextants, were the lack of rigidity of the frame and the inaccuracy of the scale. The sextant exhibited here has a reinforced brass frame and large (18-inch) radius to counteract these sources of error—but the result is a very heavy instrument. It is therefore fitted with a socket on the back of the frame so that its weight can be taken either by a tripod on the ground (when used on shore) or by a short staff resting in the waistbelt of the observer.

The hand-divided scale can be read by a vernier to one minute of arc. The tangent screw is lacking and the original telescope has been replaced by a replica.

Cook is known to have taken a very similar instrument with him on his voyages.

44. GREGORIAN REFLECTING TELESCOPE, *1770*
Inscribed Francis Watkins, Charing Cross. Focal length 24", aperture $4\frac{7}{8}$". NMG, London, England.

In sending transit observers throughout the world (as in a Geophysical Year) the special intention was to achieve uniformity of results. At Tahiti Cook and Charles Green used James Short's two-foot Gregorian reflectors. On the Second and Third Voyages similar instruments by John Bird were used to view eclipses of the sun and moon and Jupiter's satellites and occultations of stars by the moon. Cook's personal telescope on the First Voyage was a Francis Watkins, like this.

45. TELESCOPE USED IN OBSERVING THE TRANSIT OF VENUS IN AMERICA
FIS, Philadelphia.

This is also an Edward Nairne brass reflecting telescope which was used at Norriton, Pa. by Dr. William Smith, first provost of the University of Pennsylvania. With him were David Rittenhouse and John Lukens.

James Gregory developed the principle of physical and mathematical corrections for spherical and chromatic aberrations in *Optica Promota* (1663). He was not mechanically skillful however, and it was not until the mid-18th century that James Short of Edinburgh reduced the Gregorian principles to a working telescopic model. The records reveal that the transit was being observed throughout the world, and not always for scientific reasons. The French expedition in Russia produced a large atlas in Paris devoted to the Russian provinces. No doubt several expeditions carried Secret Instructions similar to Cook's.

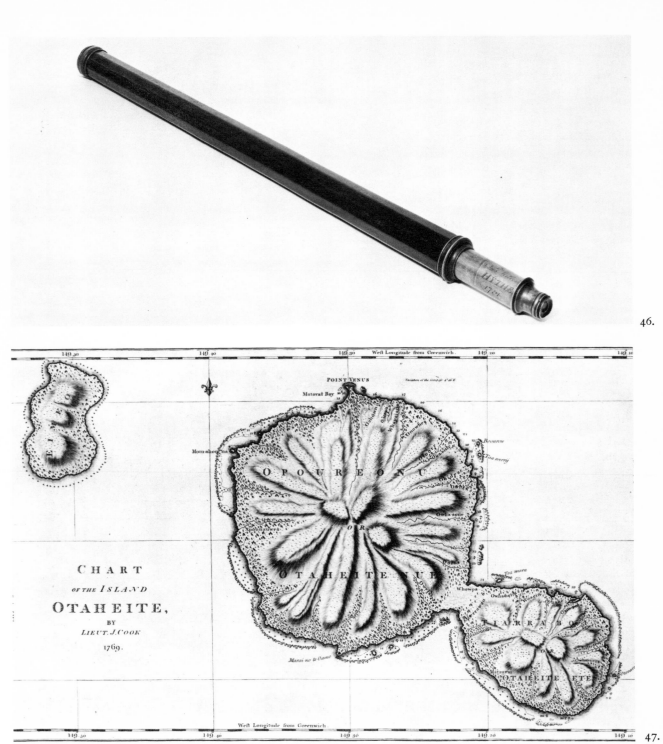

46.

CHART
OF THE ISLAND
OTAHEITE,
BY
LIEUT. J. COOK
1769.

47.

POINT VENUS

Matavai Bay

O POU REON U

OR

OTAHEITE NUE

West Longitude from Greenwich.

CAPTAIN HUGH PALLISER
By Sir Nathaniel Dance. See Cat. no. 3.

46. ACHROMATIC HAND TELESCOPE
Inscribed: Dollond London and Jno. Miller Hythe 1781. 6″ x 26″.
NMG, London.

Dollond's telescopes (about 1770) were the best available at this time. The achromatic object glass, introduced in the 1750s, rendered objects practically color-free and the telescope much more compact. The smallness of the object glass was due to the shortage of good quality optical glass at this time.

The focal length is 28 inches, the diameter of object glass, 1 inch. Courtesy NMG.

47. CHART OF TAHITI, *1769*
Chart of the Island Otaheite, by Lieut. J. Cook 1769. Engraved by J. Cheeven. 25.5″ x 18″. NMG, London.

Point Venus will be seen at the northern tip of the island, the anchor close to the westward, symbolizing the *Endeavour's* anchorage in Matavai Bay, the point to the southwest of it being One Tree Hill.

Courtesy NMG, J. Hawkesworth, 1773, Vol. 2.

48. NEW ZEALAND—*1642 to date*
Chart of New Zealand explored in 1769 and 1770, by Lieut. J. Cook, Commander of His Majesty's Bark Endeavour. Engraved by I. Bayly after J. Cook (published 1772). 24″ x 28¾″. NMG, London.

The modern overlay placed on Cook's First Voyage chart, shows in different colors the coastlines of New Zealand as they were known at various dates, with the more important modern place names. Tasman's coastline is yellow, Cook's First and Second Voyages are in black and green, and the red is from current Admiralty charts, obtained by radio time signals. Overlay prepared by Hydrographic Department, Ministry of Defense. Courtesy, NMG.

49. A CHART IN COOK'S OWN HAND, NEW SOUTH WALES, *1770*
Facsimile. 39¼″ x 21″. NMG, London.

On a copy of the chart exhibited here, almost certainly drawn by Cook himself, though neither is signed, Cook has inserted the title: "A Chart of part of the Sea Coast of New South Wales on the East Coast of New Holland From Point Hickes to Smoaky Cape by Lieut. J. Cook Commander of His Majesty's Bark the *Endeavour* 1770."

Original in British Museum. Add. MS 31360 folio 45, and Add. MS 7085, folio 35. Courtesy, NMG.

50. EAST COAST OF AUSTRALIA—*1770* AND TODAY
A chart of New South Wales on the east coast of New Holland. Engraved chart by W. Whitchurch after James Cook (published 1773 Cook Vol. 3) with modern overlay. North is to the right. 38.5″ x 21¾″. NMG.

An overlay has been placed on Cook's First Voyage chart of the east coast of Australia, showing in red the coastline as laid down on modern charts, together with the more important modern place names.

Cook "Discover'd and Explored" the whole of this coast during 1770—the first European to do so. He called it all New South Wales. Today, that name is used only for the southern part, while the northern part is Queensland. In Cook's day, the continent of Australia was known as New Holland.

Compare this engraved chart with the larger-scale manuscript chart in Cook's own hand exhibited nearby, which was the basis of the southern part of the engraved chart as published. Overlay prepared by the Hydrographic Department, Ministry of Defence.

51. PORTRAIT OF SIR JOSEPH BANKS, *Baronet, President of The Royal Society.*
By Thomas Phillips, R.A. (1770-1845). 139 x 109.3 cm. Oils on canvas. DG, LNSW, Sydney, Australia.

Banks had his portrait painted on many occasions, by such leading London artists as Sir Joshua Reynolds, the American Benjamin West, longtime President of the Royal Academy, and Sir Thomas Lawrence. Thomas Phillips, R.A., painted several, three of which are very similar. These are owned by the Royal Society, the National Portrait Gallery (London), and the Royal Horticultural Society.

The portrait exhibited was purchased in 1929 by Sir William Dixson from Captain Knatchbull-Hugessen and was painted to the order of Don Jose de Mendoza y Rios, F.R.S., as a presentation to Banks. It was engraved by N. Schiavonetti in 1812. A replica of the portrait was painted for Mendoza and bequeathed by him to the Royal Society. At least seven different engravings were made from this. After the death of Lady Banks her original came into the possession of the Knatchbull-Hugessen family; a copy was made to the order of the Captain in 1929 before he sold the painting.

52. PORTRAIT OF SIR JOSEPH BANKS
By Rembrandt Peale. Oil on canvas. PANS, Philadelphia.

Obviously Banks was a self-starter who made the best of his good fortune and intellectual gifts—and he was a man of affairs and influence all his zestful life. He had been educated at Eton, Harrow, and Oxford, with further botanical studies at Oxford.

In his twenties he was a Fellow of the Royal Society. He established the larger scheme of the First Voyage which became

55.

56.

the pattern for future voyages' combined expeditions.

He was also President of the Royal Society. Lieutenant King of the Third Voyage referred to him as "the common center of the discoveries." No wonder that a young American student of Benjamin West would be so desirous of painting the scientific lion. Later Rembrandt Peale, who was born at the time of the Third Voyage, succeeded Trumbull in 1825 as President of the American Academy of Fine Arts.

53. SIR JOSEPH BANKS (1743-1820)
President of the Royal Society.
Bust by Turnerelli in 1814 when Banks was 71 years old.
NMG, London.

Banks' career upon return from "his Pacific voyage" with Lieutenant Cook (1768-71) and a journey to Iceland was filled with adventure. He unfortunately suffers in too close association or comparison with Cook. In this bust, executed almost 50 years later, one can still see the generous exuberance and attractive energetic force which won Sir Joseph so many friends and followers. While he cannot compare with Cook, the great navigator learned much from the young peer of social as well as scientific details. It is nice to know that the coolness which prevailed for a time after the First Voyage was banished by Cook's good sense and the desire for firsthand knowledge for which Banks ever thirsted.

We are especially privileged to see here Banks at more than one stage of his eventful life. Banks was not only a Fellow of the Royal Society at a young age, but also for over 40 years the generous patron and President of the august body. Fortunately for his world and ours, and for the ever present luster of Cook, the young scientist took with him on the First Voyage scientific naturalists and botanical artists who faithfully and methodically recorded the fauna, flora, marine life, native peoples, their habitats and means of living. Through these astonishing experiences he and Cook learned much, and so, too, did the European world of learning.

When the Second and Third Voyages took place, it was only natural to include scientific and artistic recorders of the explorations.

54. JOSEPH BANKS, *Naturalist*
Mezzotint by J. R. Smith after Benjamin West, 1788.
32¼″ x 23½″. NMG, London.

Instead of the Grand Tour of European capitals then customary to complete the education of wealthy young men, Banks, at the age of 25, chose and persuaded the Admiralty to allow him to do a tour of the world by accompanying Captain Cook with a scientific entourage on his voyage to Tahiti in a once in a century opportunity to observe the Transit of Venus from the southern hemisphere.

Later, Banks created Kew Gardens and was President of the Royal Society, during which period he exercised great influence upon scientific progress in Britain. He was knighted in 1781, became a Knight of the Bath in 1795 and was admitted to the Privy Council, 1797.

55. PORTRAIT OF JOSEPH BANKS (*ca 1772*)
Engraved by J. R. Smith after the oil painting by Benjamin West, P.R.A. (1738-1820) HL, Dunedin, N.Z. 57.3 x 38 cm.
Mezzotint engraving, published 15 April 1773.

This is of particular interest when compared with the masterful Reynolds portrait of Banks, also made on his return from the First Voyage. The young gentleman of fashion is surrounded by the exotic fruits of his voyage to the South Seas. Wearing a Maori cloak, fringed with dog hair, he stands beside a carved war-staff (taisha), a canoe paddle, and other items of ethnographical interest. In the foreground is a large Polynesian adze and a folio volume of plant drawings. It is most regrettable that the original portrait in oils is lost. A further observation about this rare print is that it reappeared in 1788, with a new title recognizing that the subject was "Sir Joseph Banks, Bart., President of the Royal Society." A eulogistic Latin verse is also included.

Benjamin West was born at Springfield, Pennsylvania, of an old Quaker family from Buckinghamshire in England. At the age of 18, he set up in Philadelphia as a portrait painter. Two years later he moved to New York where he enjoyed considerable success. In 1760 friends assisted his three-year art study in Italy where he also achieved considerable reputation.

West then established himself in London with King George III as his patron. He specialized in historical subjects and in 1768 was one of the four artists who presented the King with a plan to establish the Royal Academy, of which he was a founding member. He was appointed Historical Painter to His Majesty in 1772. Twenty years later he succeeded Sir Joshua Reynolds as President of the Royal Academy, and held that position till his death. As an indication of his immense reputation, West was buried in St. Paul's Cathedral, but today the painter of "The Death of Wolfe" is less revered. Among his American students in London were John Singleton Copley, Gilbert Stuart, and Samuel F. B. Morse.

56. ORIGINAL MANUSCRIPT JOURNAL KEPT BY SIR JOSEPH BANKS, *baronet, on Cook's first voyage, in ENDEAVOUR, covering the period of 9 October 1769 to 10 October 1770, from Poverty Bay in N.Z. to Batavia.*
20 x 16 cm., 157 pp. APL, Auckland, N.Z.

The fuller complete journal kept by Banks on the First

59.

61

Voyage is in the Mitchell Library, Sydney, Australia, and this was published by that Library, edited by the late Professor J. C. Beaglehole, OM. A contemporary transcript, made for Banks' friend, Lord Mulgrave, now is in the Alexander Turnbull Library, Wellington, N.Z. It is also displayed in this Exhibition.

57. MANUSCRIPT DESCRIPTION BY SIR JOSEPH BANKS OF THE 14 ISLANDS OF THE SOCIETY ISLANDS (Tahiti), 1769, 5 pp. APL, Auckland, N.Z.

In his journal of the First Voyage Cook frequently used extracts from the journal kept by Banks, and in the published account Dr. Hawkesworth used even more of Banks rather than Cook. These descriptive passages reveal ways in which Cook learned from Banks' earlier scientific training.

MANUSCRIPT DESCRIPTION BY SIR JOSEPH BANKS OF OTAHEITE (Tahiti), 4 pp.

58. SYDNEY PARKINSON, artist (ca 1745-71)
14″ x 11¼″. NMG, London.

The most important artist of the First Voyage, he was the son of an Edinburgh brewer and apprenticed as a woolen-draper.

His skill in botanical illustration attracted the attention of Joseph Banks, who took him into his employ in 1767 and on the voyage employed him as botanical draughtsman.

1,300 drawings and sketches speak for Parkinson's industry in the face of extraordinary hazards. On Tahiti, for instance, flies were so numerous that, not only did they cover the subject, they even ate the color off the paper as fast as he could lay it on.

He was one of the 23 who died of dysentery following the Endeavour's 10 weeks' stay in Batavia for repairs. Courtesy NMG.

59. DANIEL SOLANDER, Naturalist (1733-82)
15″ x 12½″. NMG, London.

A Swede, he entered Uppsala University where he won Linnaeus' warm approval. As genial as he was industrious, Solander came to England in 1760 and, in 1763, joined the staff of the British Museum. There, in 1767, he met Banks who invited him to join the expedition as chief naturalist.

Solander later became Banks' assistant and librarian. His premature death contributed to the botanical and zoological results of this and other voyages remaining unpublished. Courtesy NMG.

60. HERMAN DIEDRICH SPÖRING, Naturalist (1730-71)
NMG, London.

Son of a Professor of Medicine at the University of Abo in Sweden (now Finland) he assisted Solander and also made a number of very competent drawings.

He died two days before Parkinson, on the 24th of January, 1771, from dysentery contracted during the stay at Batavia. No portrait of him is known.

61. ROBERT MOLYNEUX (1746-71),
Master of the ENDEAVOUR, ca 1769.
A portrait in oils on canvas by an artist unknown, HL, Dunedin, N.Z.

The Master of a vessel was a warrant officer, not a commissioned officer. As the chief professional aboard, he was responsible for the ship's navigation and for her log, among many other duties. Molyneux had sailed around the world once previously as Master's Mate in Dolphin under Wallis, 1766-68. Promoted to Master for Cook's First Voyage, Molyneux was known as an excellent chart maker. Like so many others, he contracted dysentery at Batavia and died at Capetown on the long voyage home. Endeavour left the Cape on 16 April 1771. Cook wrote in his journal: "At 4 Departed this Life Mr. Robt Molineux, a young man of good parts but had unfortunately given himself up to extravagancy and intemperance which brought on disorders that put a pirod to his life." This was perhaps harsh, since the virtuous Sydney Parkinson also succumbed.

The portrait was purchased by the Hocken Library in 1970 from Molyneux's great-great-great-nephew, Mr. P. E. Molyneux, Newburg, Berkshire, England. The handsome portrait was reproduced in the first volume of the Hakluyt Society edition of Cook's Journals, where Beaglehole commented that the identification "rests on a family tradition."

62. TIERRA DEL FUEGO (THE LAND OF FIRE), 1765
A representation of the interview between Commodore Byron and the Patagonians. 17¼″ x 23¼″. NMG, London.

Captain "Foulweather Jack" Byron landed on the Patagonian coast in the course of his voyage around the world. He reported seeing there some remarkably large men which grew from his 1765 report on Patagonian giants. This was somewhat like Pigafetta's report from the Magellan expedition and in public reception stimulated either controversy or mirth. Courtesy, NMG.

63. MATAVAI BAY FROM ONE TREE HILL, Tahiti, 1769
The tree is a new species of the Erythrina (coral tree). Engraving after S. Parkinson (1745-71). 17¼″ x 18″. NMG, London.

In the distance, Endeavour is at anchor off Fort Venus, whose tents and defenses can be seen behind the ship.

This is a remarkably faithful engraving of an unsigned pen-

65.

67.

68.

69.

and-wash drawing by Parkinson (British Museum, Add. MS
23921. 6a). From J. Hawkesworth, *An Account of the Voyages
undertaken . . . for Making Discoveries in the Southern Hemisphere*,
London (1773) Vol. 2, Pl. 2.

64. CANOES OF TAHITI, 1769
*A view in the Island of Ulietea, with a double canoe and a boat-
house. Engraving by E. Rooker, after S. Parkinson (1745?-71)
18½" x 26½". NMG, London.*

"The sailing Proes have some one and some two masts, the
sails are off Matting . . . those that go double . . . two Canoes
are placed in a parallel direction to each other about three or
four feet asunder securing them together by small logs of wood
laid across and lashed to each of their gunnels, thus the one boat
supports the other and are not in least danger of oversetting . . .
having large shades or houses to put them in built for the purpose . . ." Hawkesworth (1773), Vol. 2, Pl. 3. Cook, Journal,
12th July and 9th August, 1769.

65. A TROPICAL FISH (Chaetodon chrysostomus)
*Facsimile of watercolor drawing by Sydney Parkinson (1745?-71).
16¼" x 22¼". NMG, London.*

There are now 262 drawings of fishes from Cook's voyages
in the British Museum (Natural History), of which 156 are by
Parkinson, 78 by Forster, 15 by Ellis, 7 by Buchan and 6 by
Spöring: a further 7 by Webber are in the British Museum at
Bloomsbury. Only a small proportion of the drawings are
completed, the majority being sketches with washes of color.
They are executed in pencil, rarely crayon or ink, and are
occasionally shaded in pencil.

From S. Parkinson, Drawings of Animals, 3 volumes.

66. CUTTING FROM Erythrina indica, Tahiti, 1769
*Facsimile of a watercolor by Sydney Parkinson preserved in the
British Museum (Natural History). 26¼" x 19". NMG, London.*

This fairly large tree is found from India eastwards to
Southern Polynesia; it has a smooth gray bark, black thorns
and bears clusters of scarlet flowers after leaf fall.

67. BREADFRUIT, Tahiti, 1769
*A branch of the breadfruit tree (Artocarpus communis) with the
fruit. Engraved by J. F. Miller after S. Parkinson (1745?-71).
Engraving has been reversed from original watercolor in
British Museum. 22¼" x 19¼". NMG.*

The *Endeavour* reached Tahiti on 13 April 1769, "with but
very few men upon the Sick List and these had but slite
complaints," recorded Cook. "We had no sooner come to an
anchor . . . than a great number of natives in their Canoes came
off to the Ship and brought with them Cocoa-nuts etc . . ."

Breadfruit was evidently included in the etc. for, on 2 May,

when Cook and Green, the astronomer, "went to set up the
Quadt. (with which the Transit of Venus was to be observed)
it was not to be found, it had never been taken out of the
Packing case (which was about 18 inches square), since it came
from Mr. Bird [1709-76] the Maker, and the whole was pretty
heavy, so that it was a matter of astonishment to us all how it
could be taken away, as a Centinal stood the whole night
within 5 yards of the door of the Tent where it was put . . ."

Banks and Green having retrieved it, whilst Cook collected
and followed with an armed party, the natives took fright and
the chief, Tootaha, cut off food supplies for two days until
Cook took some steps to reconcile "this man to us in order to
procure a Sufficient supply of Bread fruit and Cocoa-nuts."

Engraving from J. Hawkesworth, 1773, Vol. 2, Pl. 11.

68. TAHITI, FLY FLAP, 1769
*16¾" x 14½". Engraving from J. Hawkesworth (1773), Pl. 12.
NMG, London, England.*

The middle figure is a fly flap from Ohiteoa and the two
side views are handles of flaps from Tahiti in one-third-inch
scale. The fly swarms of Tahiti were much commented upon.

69. STONE TOOLS, Tahiti, 1769
*Engraved by Record from artifacts taken back to England.
17" x 14½". NMG.*

The first figure, reckoning from the left hand, is an adze of
the larger size; the second and third are different representations of the upper part of it, to show the manner of tying the
stone to the handle; the smaller figures are tattooing instruments, to pierce the skin, of different sizes, with and without
their handles, the last is the instrument with which they are
struck for that purpose.

"When one considers the tools these people have to work
with one cannot but admire their workmanship, these are
Adzes and small hatchets made of a hard stone, Chisels or
gouges made of human bones . . . to plane or polish their work
they rub it with a smooth stone, Coral beat small and mixt
with water . . ." Cook Journal, 12 July, 1769.

Engraving from J. Hawkesworth (1777) Vol. 2, Pl. 10.

70. TATTOOING INSTRUMENTS, Tahiti, 1769
*Engraved by Record from artifacts taken back to England,
17" x 14½". NMG.*

"Both sexes paint their bodys Tattow as it is called in their
language, this is done by inlaying the Colour of black under
their skins in such manner as to be indelible . . . The Colour
they use is lamp black . . . the Instruments for pricking it under
the skin is made of very thin flat pieces of [b]one or shell . . .
one end is cut into sharp teeth . . . this is a painfull operation."

The first sailor to inaugurate the long and noble tradition of the tattooed sailor appears to have been Able Seaman Stainsby of the *Adventure*. Parkinson and two others also had their arms marked. It was painful.

Engraving from J. Hawkesworth (1777), Vol. 2, Pl. 9.

71. MAORI WEAPONS, 1769
Bludgeons, used as weapons by the New Zealanders, and called PATU-PATUS as seen on the side, the edge, and the end. They are from 14 to 18 inches long, and broad and thick in proportion. Engraved by Record after an original pen and wash drawing probably made by J. K. Miller (fl 1768-85), from artifacts taken back to England. 15½" x 16½". NMG, London.

"Strange that with such a war like people . . . no Omissive weapons are found among them such as Bows and Arrows, Slings etc . . . The Arms they use are long spears . . . short Truncheons . . . Pattoo Pattooes, some made of wood some of bone and others of stone . . . the use of these is to knock men's brains out . . . Besides . . . they throw stones and darts . . . 10 or 12 feet long . . . of hard wood." Cook, Journal, 12th November, 1769.

These weapons, like the defensive fortifications, were all made at immense cost of labor with the aid of stone and bone tools only.

Engraving from J. Hawkesworth (1773), Vol. 3, Pl. 14.

72. MAORI WAR CANOE, 1769
A war canoe of New Zealand, with a view of Gable End Foreland. Engraving after S. Parkinson (1745-71). No engraver noted. 16" x 29".

"The People show great ingenuity and good workmanship in the building and framing their Boats or Canoes; the[y] are longer and narrow . . . Their large canoes are I believe built wholy for war and will carry 40 to 80 or 100 men with their arms, etc. . . . Length 68½ feet, breadth 5 feet and depth 3½ feet . . . well fastened together with strong plating . . .

The ornaments . . . were of carved work . . . and birds feathers." Cook Journal, March 31st, 1770.

The unknown engraver "stretched" the smaller canoe shown in a Parkinson pen and wash drawing, to depict the larger one referred to by Cook.

Engraving from J. Hawkesworth (1773), Vol. 3, Pl. 16.

73. A MAORI FORTRESS, 1769 .
A fortified town or village, called a Hippah, built on a perforated rock at "Tolaga in New Zealand." Engraving after H. D. Sporing (ca 1730-71). No engraver noted. 17¼" x 18¼". NMG, London.

Whereas the Polynesians of the islands lived in scattered houses, the Maoris of New Zealand lived in scattered fortified villages of as many as 500 houses. The great fortified pa (hippah) was unknown elsewhere in the Pacific: ". . . the Villages are built upon eminences near the Sea, and are fortified on the land side with a Bank and a Ditch, and Pallisaded all round . . . another of these small fortified Rocks . . . communicates with the Main by a narrow pathway where there is a small village . . ." Cook Journal, 2nd and 12th November, 1769.

Actually this scene is at Mercury Bay, on the Coromandel Peninsula, further north, but it was also wrongly located in Parkinson's own *Journal*.

Engraving from J. Hawkesworth (1773), Vol. 2, Pl. 18.

74. A KANGAROO, ENDEAVOUR RIVER, AUSTRALIA, 1770
An animal found on the coast of New Holland called Kanguroo. An engraving after a drawing by S. Parkinson (1745-71). 16¾" x 18". NMG, London.

The discovery of anything seen for the first time is an occasion of excitement—land, flowers, and plants, stars or strange fishes. Yet imagine Saturday, 23 June, the *Endeavour* laid up on shore after a narrow escape on the reef and then: ". . . one of the men saw an animal something less than a grey hound, it was of a Mouse Colour very slender made and swift of foot."

Then the next day Cook saw it: ". . . of a light Mouse colour and the full size of a grey hound . . . with a long tail . . . it jumped like a Hare or a dear . . ." to which Cook later added: "its progression is by hoping (sic) or jumping for 8 feet at each hop upon its hind legs only . . ." Such excitement!

British Museum (Natural History) Parkinson's Drawings 1, 3, 4.

75. TRUNCHEON OR PATU, *Maori. NMG, London.*
12th Nov., 1769. "They have short Truncheons about a foot long, which they call Pattoo Pattoos, some made of wood some of bone and others of stone, those made of wood are variously shaped, but those made of bone and stone are of one shape, which is with a round handle a broadish blade which is thickest in the middle and tapers to an edge all round, the use of these are to knock mens brains out and to kill them outright after they are wounded: and they are certainly well contrived things for this purpose." Cook, Journal.

76. MAORI CLUB-AXE, *Tewhatewha* NMG, London.
A similar weapon is depicted being brandished by a Maori warrior in a war canoe in a pen-and-wash drawing by Sydney

80.

81.

Parkinson, the artist carried in *Endeavour* on the first voyage (1768-71).

12th Nov. 1769. "The Arms they use are Long spears or lances, a staff . . . another sort about 4½ feet long, these are shaped at one end like an Axe and the other end is made with a sharp point." Cook, Journal.

The blow was struck not with the edge of the blade, but with its thick back. This club is reputed to have been collected by Cook during his Second Voyage.

77. MAORI WAR STAFF, OR TAIAHA
NMG, London.

(November, 1769) "The Arms they use are Long spears or lances, a Staff about 5 feet long, some of these are painted at one end like a Sergeants Halbard others are round and sharp, the others ends are broad something like the blade of an oar . . ." Cook, Journal. Courtesy, NMG.

77 a, b, c. THREE TAHITIAN PIECES FROM THE FIRST VOYAGE (1769)
Originally in Trinity College Collection, now Sandwich Collection, CAM, Cambridge, England.
77 (a). A simple mahogany head rest, Tahiti (1769).

77 (b). A heavy barkcloth or tapa mallet (beater) made of iron-wood with varied treatment of surfaces for different stages of pulping manufacture finished out with an ornamental treatment of end (1769).

77 (c). A tapa cloth brought back from the First Voyage.

78. THE SOUTH SEAS CIRCUMNAVIGATED, 1772-75.
A Chart of the Southern Hemisphere showing the Tracks of some of the most distinguished Navigators by Captain James Cook. 29.5″ x 31″. NMG, London.

In the postscript to his first *Journal*, Cook had put forward the tentative plan for a further Pacific voyage. He had learned the need for a base for refitting in distant seas as secure as Plymouth at home, the need to explore the southern Pacific in high latitudes in summer, using the prevailing winds from the west, and the need in consequence to enter and leave it by sailing eastwards.

In November, 1771, Cook was commissioned to command such an expedition with two ships, like the *Endeavour* former east coast colliers, soon to be called the *Resolution* and *Adventure*. Courtesy, NMG.

79. CHART OF THE SOUTH PACIFIC, 1773.
Chart of Part of the South Seas, showing the Track and Discoveries made by all the ships. Engraved by W. Whitechurch,

Pleasant Row, Islington. 30″ x 23″. NMG.

The longitude, it will be seen, is measured from Greenwich and not as was customary till then, from London. This is because the longitudes were determined by lunar distances using *The Nautical Almanac for 1769*, whose tables were based upon the meridian line passing through the transit instrument in the Royal Observatory in Greenwich Park. Courtesy, NMG.

From J. Hawkesworth, *An Account of the Voyages Undertaken . . . for Making Discoveries in the Southern Hemisphere*, London, 1773. 3 volumes (Vol. 1).

80. SCALE MODEL OF HMS *RESOLUTION*
The former cat-built Whitby collier Marquis of Granby.
OHS, Portland, Oregon.

The so aptly named HMS *Resolution*, 462 tons, was selected by Cook who said: ". . . she was the ship of my choice and as I thought the fittest for the Service . . ." Whatever her name, the apple-cheeked hull was strong in every respect and a very familiar kind of bluff bowed vessel, ideal for Cook's work as was *Adventure*.

This model for which the lines were taken off by Hewitt Jackson, Esq. and the research done by him in company with Edmund Hayes, Chairman of the Exhibition, is thought to be the finest model of *Resolution* extant. The original is 110′ 8″ by 35′ 5½″ maximum by 13′ 1½″ depth of hold.

The model was built by Eric Pardy of Seattle and given to the Maritime Collection of the Oregon Historical Society Museum by the Chairman at a dedication on December 1, 1972.

81. THE FOREPART OF THE SMALL WOODEN FIGUREHEAD *of HMS RESOLUTION* (462 tons).
The former cat-built Whitby collier Marquis of Granby, *was re-rigged as a sloop-of-war for Cook's Second and Third Voyages of 1772-75 and 1776-80. NMW, Wellington, N.Z. from permanent Cook display there.*

The creature is a Talbot, a heraldic representation of a hound or hunting dog. There was a variety of hound called Talbot after the noble Irish family of that name, used for tracking and hunting, as it had great powers of scent. Such would be a highly appropriate device for Cook's ship in her wide-ranging explorations. According to the Committee it is also the name of an estimable claret.

The authenticity of the figurehead is vouched for by its having come from the estate of Admiral Isaac Smith, Mrs. Cook's cousin, being purchased in 1831 by the 5th Viscount Galway, together with the portrait of Captain Clerke. Both items were presented to New Zealand in 1941 by the retiring Governor-General of that country, the 8th Lord Galway.

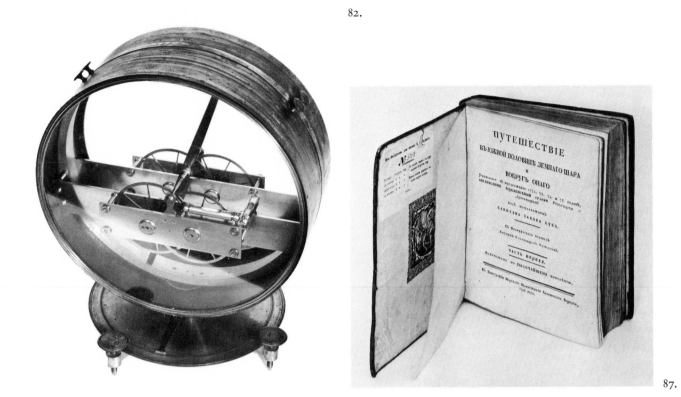

82.

87.

83.

82. DIPPING NEEDLE, *1772*

Inscribed Nairne, London. 13" x 16". NMG, London.

Said to have been taken on Cook's Second Voyage.

"In the year 1772, Mr. Nairne completed two dipping needles for the Board of Longitude, agreeably to a plan of the Rev. Mr. Mitchell, a gentleman eminently distinguished for his great knowledge in magnetics." Rees, *Cyclopaedia*, London, 1819.

The dipping needle measures the vertical component of the earth's magnetic field in the same way that the compass needle indicates the horizontal component. The magnetized needle in both cases is aligned along the line of force of the earth's magnetic field in the plane in which it is free to move.

Cook and his scientists observed the dip of the needle at various positions on the earth's surface during his Second and Third Voyages and several references occur in his journals. For the Third Voyage, the instrument was redesigned to eliminate various defects which became apparent during the previous voyage.

The magnetized needle is 12 inches in length, pivoted on four friction wheels. The ends of the axis of the needle, and also the friction wheels, are made of an alloy of gold and copper, and bear upon end-plates of polished agate.

The circular scale reads to half a degree and is made of silvered bell metal, the whole enclosed in a brass and glass case to prevent disturbance by the wind. Two spirit levels are provided and the instrument is levelled by means of four screws set in the base. Courtesy NMG.

83. ALEXANDER HOOD'S SURVEYING INSTRUMENTS: COMPASS, PROTRACTOR, RULER AND SPIRIT-LEVEL, *Made of boxwood and brass*
NLA, Canberra, Australia.

Alexander Hood (1758-98) was the son of a purser in the Royal Navy and a first cousin to Admiral Lord Hood (for whom Mount Hood was named) and Lord Bridport. He sailed in *Resolution* on the Second Voyage, aged 14, as an Able-Bodied Seaman. On 6 April 1774 he was the first to sight land in the Marquesas and Cook named Hood Island in honor of him. Hood subsequently served in the West Indies and North America, being promoted to Captain in 1781. Beaglehole also records that from 1790 Hood was employed in the English Channel in the long Napoleonic Wars. While commanding HMS *Mars* (76 guns) he was killed in a desperate action against the French ship *Hercule*, in April 1798.

Hood Island was the large rock, Fatu Huku, in the southeastern group of the Marquesas. Hood's Journal, 5 March 1772-10 March 1775, is in the Admiralty records. "It is carefully written, without originality of phrase," reports Beaglehole.

84. VOYAGE ROUND THE WORLD

Manuscript journals of William Bayly, Astronomer with Captain Cook on Second and Third Voyages. 2 Vols.
ATL, Wellington, N.Z.

Journal kept on board HMS *Adventure*, June 22, 1772 to July 14, 1774. Journal kept on board HMS *Discovery*, June 11, 1776 to April 29, 1779. Journal of Narrative Occurrences, during Captain Cook's stay at Otaheite, or the Society Islands, Christmas Island and Sandwich Islands, during the time from his arrival at Otaheite, August 12, 1777 to June 30, 1778.

Bayly was assistant to William Wales, and we can be grateful to him for a faithful albeit uninspired record. He too was a farm boy from Wiltshire.

85. COOK TO VICTUALLING OFFICE

Original letter of May 30, 1772, to the Commissioners of Victualling at the Admiralty. NLA, Canberra

86. COOK TO VICTUALLING OFFICE, *February 19, 1772*
NLA, Canberra.

In which Cook informs the "Honble Gentlemen" that His Majesty's Sloops the *Resolution* and *Adventure* plan "to take in the whole of the Spirits and Wine demanded" when they touch at Portsmouth as they leave on the Second Voyage.

87. RUSSIAN TRANSLATION OF COOK'S SECOND VOYAGE. *1796, Vol. I of four volumes.*
ATL, Wellington, N.Z.

When the three research voyages were completed they were almost immediately recorded officially as well as in illegal and pirated publications and translated into all of the languages—French, Italian, German, Russian—and others. This handsome Russian volume was done as *A Journey to the Southern Half of the Globe* etc., published by the Naval Academy (St. Petersburg) and translated (from the French edition) by L. G. Kutuzov. Mrs. Cook, who lived 54 years beyond her husband, received an annual income from some of these publications.

88. MANUSCRIPT LETTER OF 27 SEPTEMBER 1775, FROM HENRY J. MORRIS TO SIR JAMES WRIGHT
APL, Auckland, N.Z. 3 pp.

Refers to a manuscript, apparently in Dutch, relating to Abel Tasman's first discovery of New Zealand in December, 1642, which Wright had sent Norris for analysis. Norris compares some of the conclusions reached by Tasman and Cook in respect of the positions of various places visited by both.

89. WILLIAM HODGES, R.A., *Artist (1744-97)*
From a drawing by George Dance March 10, 1793. Lent to NMG by Royal Academy of Arts, London. 20¾" x 17¼". NMG.

A version was engraved by William Daniell (1769-1837)

90.

93.

91.

and published by him in August 1810.

Hodges was the official artist on board *Resolution* during the Second Voyage and the pictures he painted became the property of the Lords Commissioners of the Admiralty who engaged him. He also acted in some respects as the modern press photographer, for not only did he exhibit a number of his pictures at the Royal Academy after his return but many were engraved and published to reach a far wider public, both at home and abroad. The brilliance of his work is even today insufficiently recognized.

90. THE FORSTERS, *Naturalists*
Johann and his son George at Tahiti. From an engraving by D. Beyel after J. F. Rigaud. 17¼″ x 13½″. NMG.

Johann Reinhold Forster (1729-98) and his son George (1754-94) were selected as natural historians for Cook's Second Voyage. Joseph Banks had withdrawn with his team of artists and scientists because the accommodation to be provided was inadequate. Johann Forster was an able but irascible scholar, linguist and naturalist, and a Fellow of the Royal Society. Cook found him trying. He quarrelled with William Wales, the *Resolution* astronomer and then with the Admiralty.

After the voyage Johann Forster published *Observations made during a Voyage Round the World* (London, 1778) wherein he declared: "My object was nature in its greatest extent . . . and more particularly that class of Beings to which we ourselves belong" (p. ii). He was a pioneer in social anthropology.

George Forster also discussed primitive peoples in his very readable *A Voyage Round the World* (London, 1777). He later became Professor of Natural History at Cassel and Vilnius (Wilna) and subsequently librarian to the Elector of Mayence. He was executed at Paris in 1794 for having led the Rhineland revolution the previous year. There are three botanical and two zoological volumes of his drawings and sketches in the British Museum (Natural History).

The interest of the Forsters in atmospheric effects and climate influenced Hodges' rendering of land and seascapes.

The oil painting of the Forsters by Rigaud was exhibited at the Royal Academy in 1781, with the title: "Portrait of Dr. Forster and his son on the island of Otaheite."

91. "CAPTAIN COOK'S SHIPS HMS *RESOLUTION* AND *ADVENTURE* IN THE LONG REACH, 1772"
By Francis Holman (fl 1760-90). Oil on canvas. DG, LNSW, Sydney, Australia.

Beaglehole points out that this splendid painting of Cook's ships in the Downs, 26-27 June 1772, just before the Second Voyage commenced, shows each vessel twice—broadside, with *Resolution* center and *Adventure* far right; and again, both in

stern view, at the far left. At the right in the distance is the sloop, HMS *Scorpion* to which Cook was so briefly commissioned between the First and Second Voyages. At the left foreground is the yacht of Sir George Savile, M.P., F.R.S, Vice-. President of the Society of Arts. Holman was a marine painter who specialized in shipping portraits of East Indiamen and reconstructions of major naval actions. He exhibited at the Free Society of Artists 1767-72 and at the Royal Academy 1767-84.

92. SPRING HARE: Pedetes capensis
CAPE OF GOOD HOPE. *From an unsigned watercolor drawing made at the Cape of Good Hope by G. Forster 28¾″ x 22″. NMG.*

The MS. note in ink and G. Forster on the recto is in the handwriting of Dryander, the librarian to Joseph Banks, British Museum (Natural Hsitory) Zoological Library.

93. "A VIEW IN DUSKY BAY, NEW ZEALAND,"
April, 1773
Oil on circular wooden panel by William Hodges, R.A. 25″ diam. ACAG, Auckland, N.Z.

In his journal Cook wrote, at Dusky Sound, on Monday, 12 April 1773: "Being a fine afternoon, I took Mr. Hodges to a large Cascade . . . He took a drawing of it on paper and afterwards painted it in oyle Colours which exhibits at one view a better discription of it than I can give . . ." The Maori was one of a small family, who had taken refuge from their enemies in the remote forests of the west coast of the South Island. "During our stay with them, Mr. Hodges made drawings of them . . ."

Since this small painting is on wood it was quite possibly painted at Dusky Sound by Hodges. One of his few New Zealand works outside the Admiralty collections, it was purchased in London by the Auckland gallery for 1,000 pounds in 1961. A large oil of the waterfall mentioned by Cook, with the Maori family, painted by Hodges at the Admiralty in 1775, includes this same figure. The engraving published in the account of this voyage, "A Family at Dusky Bay," derives from a different sketch by Hodges.

94. THE FLEET OF OTAHEITE ASSEMBLED AT OPAREE
Engraving by W. Woollett after W. Hodges. Published February 1st, 1777, by Wm. Strahan & Thos. Cadell. 16″ x 29″. NMG, London.

Saturday 14th (May, 1774) ". . . coming round the Point of Oparre . . . they approached the shore . . . in divisions of three or four or more lashed close . . . it was a pleasure to see how well they were conducted, they Paddled in . . . one after the other . . . for the Shore with all their might . . . they closed the

96.

97.

CAPTAIN CHARLES CLERKE
By Sir Nathaniel Dance. See Cat. no. 128.

line a Shore to an inch . . . This Fleet consisted of Forty sail . . . and were come to Oparre to be reviewd before Otou . . . who was present . . ." Cook, Journal.

Tu (Otou) had risen to power in the district of Matavai Bay and Pare as a result of deaths and warfare since Cook's departure from Tahiti in 1769. When Cook met him in August the year before he thought "him to be a timerous Prince."

In Admiralty House, London, is a vast oil by Hodges of this occasion. J. Cook (1777), Pl. 16.

95. THE ISLAND OF OTAHEITE BEARING S.E. DISTANT ONE LEAGUE
Engraved by W. Watts after W. Hodges (1744-97).
Published February 1st, 1777 by Wm. Strahan & Thos. Cadell.
18½" x 26½". NMG.

"Their Canoes or Proes are built all of them very narrow and some of the largest are 60 or 70 feet long . . . the pieces in which they are built are well fitted and fasten'd or sew'd together with strong platting . . . with high curv'd sterns . . . The smaller Canoes are built after the same Plan . . . In order to prevent them from oversetting when in the water all those that go single . . . have . . . out-riggers which . . . project out on one side . . ." Cook, Journal, July, 1769.

The double-hulled canoe was remarkably stable and capable of speeds of 9 to 10 knots under sail.

The single outrigger canoe evolved from the double outrigger, which originated in southeast Asia, but was unsuitable for sailing in exposed seas because of the dangerous drag effect of the leeward outrigger if forced under water. The single outrigger, when to leeward, could be counterbalanced by the crew. Courtesy NMG.

Engraving from J. Cook (1777), Pl. 53.

96. BEARDED PENGUIN, *(1772-73)*—Pygoscelis antarctica
From an unsigned painting of a penguin against a background of sea and ice, made in December 1772 or January 1773 by G. Forster.
26½" x 21". NMG.

A MS. note on verso reads: "*Aptenodytes antarctica* Indian Ocean South of Kerguelens Land."

The MS. note in ink on the recto and G. Forster is in the handwriting of Dryander, Joseph Banks' librarian, who cataloged these drawings while they were in the Banks library.

The original is in the British Museum (Natural History) Zoological Library.

97. "THE *RESOLUTION* AND *ADVENTURE* IN THE SOUTHERN OCEAN," *ca 1776*
By Thomas Luny (1759-1837). 64.4 x 96.8 cm. Oil on canvas.
ML, LNSW, Sydney, Australia.

Painted in 1781, this picture must have been based on sketches made by Hodges on the Second Voyage. There are few paintings that show both ships clearly. Luny was a marine painter, probably a pupil of Holman. He appears to have served the Royal Navy until paralysis forced his retirement in 1810. He continued to paint until his death, by which time he was very wealthy. Many of his works were engraved. He is best known for his oil painting of a cat-built Whitby bark reputed to be the *Earl of Pembroke,* later rechristened as His Britannic Majesty's bark, *Endeavour.*

98. MONUMENTS IN EASTER ISLAND
Engraving by W. Woollett after W. Hodges.
Published February 1, 1777, by W. Strahan and Thos. Cadell.
17½" x 22¼". NMG, London.

Sunday 13th (March, 1774) "In stretching for the land we discovered people and those Moniments or Idols mentioned by . . . Roggeweins . . . which left us no room to doubt but it was Easter Island . . . there is hardly an Island in this sea which affords less refreshments and conveniences for Shipping . . ." Cook, Journal.

Easter Island was discovered in 1722 by the Dutch explorer Jacob Roggeveen. Cook reached it after penetrating to latitude 71° 10' S on 30th January. He found it by running down its reported latitude. Scurvy was affecting some of the crew so that its lack of resources was a keen disappointment. Cook, with an infection of the gall bladder he never mentioned, was too ill to land.

Woollett's engraving epitomized, for a wide public, the view that the monuments were the records of a decayed civilisation. Thus, the solitary native resting on his staff contemplates, in true neo-classical manner, the symbols of mortality. Hodges' brilliant oils of the scene are in Admiralty House, London. The engraver has destroyed the majestic dignity of the original. J. Cook (1777) Pl. 49.

99. RESOLUTION BAY, MARQUESAS, *1774*
Resolution Bay in the Marquesas (at St. Christina).
Engraving by B. T. Pouncy after W. Hodges (1744-97).
Published February 1st, 1777, by Wm. Strahan & Thos. Cadell.
17½" x 22½". NMG, London.

"Their canoes are made of wood and pieces of the Bark of a soft wood . . . they are from 16 to 20 feet long and about 15 inches broad . . . the Stern rises . . . in an irregular direction and ends in a point, the head projects out horizontally . . . They are rowed with Paddles and some have a sort of Lateen sail made of Mating." Cook, Journal, 13 April, 1774.

The sails are quite distinctive in shape. The canoes had outriggers also. Besides heavy and deadly clubs, and spears, the

102.

103.

Marquesans had slings with which they threw stones "with great velocity and to a great distance but not with a good aim." J. Cook, Pl. 35.

100. BOATS OF THE FRIENDLY ISLES, 1773
Engraving by W. Watts after W. Hodges. 17" x 23". NMG.

After leaving Tahiti Cook visited the southern group of the Tonga Islands in October, 1773, and the northern groups in June, a year later.

"Nothing shows their ingenuity so much as the manner in which their Canoes are built . . . long and narrow with out riggers and built of several pieces . . . sew'd together with platting made of the outside fibres of Cocoanutts . . . all in the inside . . . those that are intended for sailing are a great deal larger . . . Two such canoes they fasten together (leaving a space of about (6) feet between them) . . . over them is laid a boarded platform . . . they are sailed with a Lateen-sail . . . of Matting . . ."

It seems probable that the lateen sail originated in East Asia in the first millennium B.C. and spread thence east to the Pacific and west to the Mediterranean. Courtesy NMG.

J. Cook (1777), Pl. 42.

101. THE LANDING AT MIDDLEBURGH ONE OF THE FRIENDLY ISLES
Engraving by J. K. Sherwin after W. Hodges.
Published February 1st, 1777, by Wm. Strahan & Thos. Cadell, London. Cook (1777), Pl. 54. 18¼" x 26¼". NMG, London.

Eua, called by Tasman "Middleburg" when he discovered it in 1643, was the first of the Tongan or Friendly Islands visited by Cook after his first winter visit to Tahiti. He reached there on 2nd October, 1773.

The engravings of the *Landings at Mallicolo* (Malekula), *Erramanga* (Eromanga) *and Tana* (Tanna, Pari) *in the New Hebrides,* were all done with almost photographic accuracy of composition from paintings by Hodges. Although the postures of his figures are quite vibrant with action, he gave so little anatomical detail that the figures were re-drawn by a figure artist from Hodges' sketches for him to copy in his oils.

Thus, G. B. Cipriani, R.A. (1728-85) made a pen-and-wash drawing of the figures for the landing at Eromanga (of which a faithful rendering of the composition was made by Hodges), but it has anatomically exact figures showing, for instance, the muscling of the men (see original from PAC on display here). The engraving of Middleburg does not seem to have an oil painting counterpart extant, although the Mitchell Library, Sydney, holds the Cipriani figure-study for the scene. George Forster's scathing strictures on these works greatly offended Hodges:

"Mr. Hodges designed this memorable interview in an elegant picture, which has been engraved for Captain Cooks account of this voyage . . . the execution of Mr. Sherwin cannot be too much admired . . . But it is greatly to be feared that Mr. Hodges has lost the sketches . . . from Nature . . . and supplied the deficiency in this case, from his own elegant ideas."

102. THE LANDING AT MALEKULA, ONE OF THE NEW HEBRIDES, 1774.
The Landing at Mallicolo, one of the New Hebrides.
Engraving by J. Basire after W. Hodges. Published February 1st, 1777 by Wm. Strahan & Thos. Cadell, London. Original oil at NMG with Landing at Tanna. 19" x 26½". NMG, London.

After his second winter visit to Tahiti Cook went, by way of the northern Tongan group, farther west to the New Hebrides where he explored in July and August, 1774. He landed first at Mallicolo (Malekula). Here he met for the first time the physically distinctive Melanesians, of whom the men went virtually naked.

The Spanish navigator Quiros had discovered these islands in 1606. J. Cook (1777), Pl. 60.

103. (a) PRELIMINARY FIGURE STUDY by Giovanni Battista Cipriani, R.A. (1728-85) London, for William Hodges to copy in his oil painting of Cook's landing at the island of Eromanga in the New Hebrides, made in London (ca 1776) after his sketch taken on the spot in July, 1774, 24.8 x 39 cm. Sepia wash, pen and ink and pencil on paper. PAC, Ottawa.

(b) "THE LANDING AT ERRAMANGA ONE OF THE NEW HEBRIDES: *painted by W. Hodges, engraved by J. K. Sherwin,*" *ATL, Wellington, N.Z. Hand-colored copperplate engraving (Pl. LXII) from the official account of Cook's Second Voyage (London, 1777).*

Cipriani was a noted artist of the day who, like others, was frequently employed by fellow artists to execute the figure work for their paintings. Hodges was placed in an embarrassing position when the classical poses of the natives in his four "Landings" engravings were harshly criticized as being unrealistic. His oil painting, probably done at the Admiralty after the voyage, is now on loan therefrom to the National Maritime Museum at Greenwich. His other pictures of "Landings" were of Malekula and Tanna, also in the New Hebrides, and Middleburg Island (now called Eua) in the Tongan group. In the Mitchell Library, Sydney, Australia, an unsigned watercolor drawing of the "Landing at Middleburg" is probably another study by Cipriani made by him for Hodges to use in his oil painting.

One cannot help but note the superb handling of the well

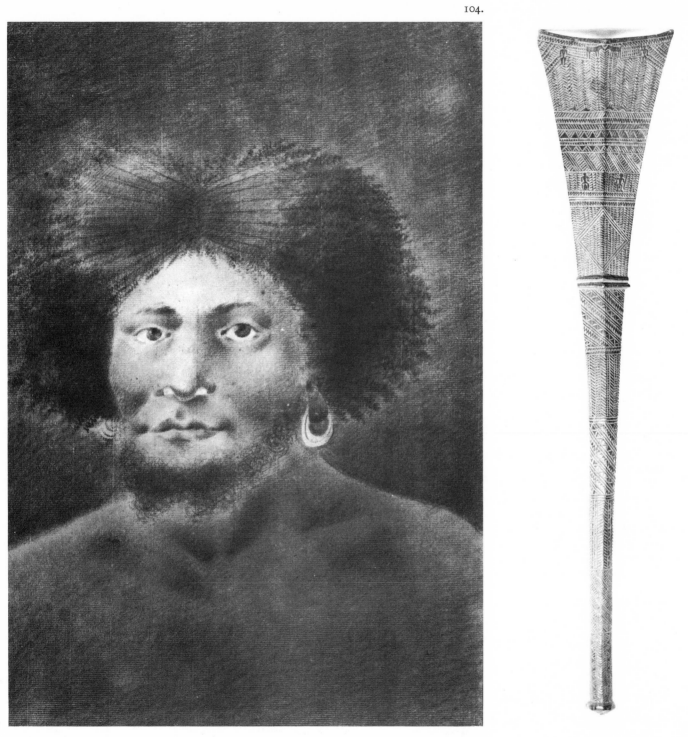

endowed natives, vigorous and classical in form as opposed to the somewhat rude looking sailors being so effectively repelled. Notable too is the extraordinary amount of background detail which seldom comes through in reproduction.

104. "A MAN OF TANNA," PORT RESOLUTION, NEW HEBRIDES, *August, 1776*
Drawing in red chalk by William Hodges, R.A. 14″ x 21″.
ATL, Wellington, N.Z.

Espiritu Santo (known to many Americans and New Zealanders during World War II) was the first of the New Hebrides group to be discovered, by the Spaniard Quiros in 1606. Bougainville, the French explorer after whom the flowering climber is named, found more islands in 1768 and called the group the Great Cyclades. But it was Cook who gave the name New Hebrides when he charted some of the islands in 1774, including Tanna, before sailing on to discover both New Caledonia and Norfolk Island. This strong picture was probably worked up in London by Hodges about 1776 from charcoal sketches made on the voyage. The picture was purchased at auction at Sotheby's in London early in 1973 (£700) by the Alexander Turnbull Library Endowment Trust.

105. "A SAVAGE OF NEW CALEDONIA IN THE ATTITUDE OF THROWING A SPEAR
Drawn by J. Webber. Engrav'd by A. W. Warren."
17.3 x 12.4 cm., engraving. DL, LNSW, Sydney, Australia

This engraving is something of an enigma. Cook discovered New Caledonia in September, 1774 on the Second Voyage and did not return there on the Third, so Webber could never have seen a native of that island. He may have copied a sketch by Hodges, or the publisher of the engraving may have wrongly attributed it to Webber instead of Hodges. In the Dixson Library is an unfinished watercolor unsigned and undated, attributed to Webber because it bears the same title, faintly in pencil. DL collections has a second engraving, by Davenport, titled "Man of New Caledonia throwing the spear."

106. STRAW-COVERED BOX, *Tahiti*
NMG, London.

This box (ca 1774) was given by Captain Cook to Mrs. Taylor of Bath, and Grosvenor Place, London, during his short stay in England before sailing in 1776 on his Third Voyage. The Taylors, a wealthy family interested in the arts and geography, were friends of Thomas Gainsborough.

The box is reputed to have been collected by Cook at Tahiti during the Second Voyage (1772-75). Courtesy, NMG.

107. WEAPONS FROM THE SOUTH SEAS

NMG, London.

The hand club (17″ x 3″), two carved war clubs (39″ x 8″ and 56″ x 8″) and spear (85″ x 1″) are all reputed to have been collected in the South Seas by crew members of Cook's Second and Third Voyages.

108. BOW, *Tierra del Fuego, First Voyage*
CAM, Cambridge, England.

On the First Voyage Cook made a deliberate coasting down South America stopping in Rio de Janeiro in December, then south toward Tierra del Fuego where this crude wooden bow was acquired.

The immediate impression is one of simplicity representing the primitive material culture of the hard pressed natives below Patagonia. By the very nature of their scarce holdings, this bowl is of excessive rarity, perhaps from the five-day stay at the Bay of Good Success halfway through the Strait. On shore Cook found ". . . perhaps as miserable a set of People as are this day upon Earth." 16 January, 1769.

109. WOODEN PATU, *Sandwich Collection*
CAM, Cambridge, England.

This patu club or *wakahika*, war club, holds comparative interest when compared with clubs of the Northwest Coast in quality of workmanship. From the First or Second Cook Voyages.

110. WARRIOR'S BELT OF FLAX, *from New Zealand*
Sandwich Collection, CAM, Cambridge, England.

A flax woven warrior's belt for which there is no association other than the First or Second Voyages. The difference would only be a design influence one might perceive in a Second Voyage specimen resulting from native contact with Europeans on the occasion of trades and thefts among First Voyage sailors.

111. TONGAN WAR CLUB, *1773*
CAM, Cambridge, England.

A magnificent 94.5 cm. in length, 19.4 cm. in largest circumference, Tonganese (ceremonial) war club acquired in 1773 in outstanding condition. This Second Voyage piece is of exceptional workmanship, exhibiting advanced dynamic designs of combat from the so-called "stone age culture." They represent what appear to be stylized scenes of combat with armed human figures in repeats. The strength and rhythms of the design combine both geometric pattern and figure and clearly reveal the attraction of such basic designs today.

112. THE NORTH PACIFIC, *1600 to date*

113.

116.

117.

Engraved chart after J. Cook and J. King. 40½" x 27". NMG.

A modern overlay placed on the chart published after Cook's Third Voyage shows in different colors the northern Pacific coastlines as they were known to Tasman and Cook, and today. Cook and King (1784), Vol. II, Pl. 36; overlay by Hydrographic Department, Ministry of Defense. Courtesy, NMG.

113. STEERING COMPASS
Inscribed: G. Adams 60 Fleet Street London G. Knight Inv. and (on the card): 1776. 10" x 10". NMG.

This compass (ca 1780) was made using Dr. Gowin Knight's flat bar needle mounted on a mica card. The compass bowl is not mounted in gimbals but pivots on a spike in the bottom of the compass box and is steadied by a pin and slide. The box is original. Courtesy, NMG.

114. VARIATION COMPASS
Inscribed: Royal Society 39. Probably by Edward Nairne of London. NMG.

The Variation compass (ca 1780) was designed to show the daily and yearly variation of a magnetic needle from true north upon land. The earth's constantly changing magnetic field was not fully understood at this time but was being investigated systematically by men like Cook and his scientists in many parts of the world.

This is not an instrument used afloat, so the box can be shallow and the scale need only measure up to 20° either side of zero.

The needle is 12 inches in length, fitted with brass slides as counterpoises and suspended by an agate cap upon a steel point. Courtesy, NMG. (Lent by the Royal Society.)

115. AZIMUTH COMPASS
Inscribed: "R. Rust & R. Eyre ye Minories LONDON." 12" x 12". NMG, London.

Similar to the compass designed by Dr. Gowin Knight for taking compass bearings of terrestrial objects and of the sun, it incorporates all his earlier improvements and is fitted with open sights and a shadow pin attachment (ca 1785).

A Knight azimuth compass, said to have been used by Captain Cook, is in the Mitchell Library, Sydney, Australia.

Gowin Knight's compasses were made by George Adams, each instrument being tested and certified by Knight himself, who signed and numbered the back of the compass card. After Knight's death in 1772, the certification of compasses was carried out by J. H. de Magalhaens. Adams continued to make the compasses until 1782, when it is thought that Rust and Eyre took over their manufacture. Courtesy, NMG.

116. 15-INCH HADLEY'S SEXTANT

Inscribed: Ramsden, London 842. 18" x 17". NMG, London.

This sextant (ca 1785) is of a slightly later date than the 15-inch Ramsden one that Cook had with him, but is similar in construction. Courtesy, NMG.

117. TENT OBSERVATORY, *1772*
A replica of a design by William Bayly. The walls are drawn back to show the interior. The large tripod for lifting off the roof (see adjacent engraving) has been omitted for reasons of space. NMG, London.

Whenever ships remained in harbor for any length of time, the astronomer would go ashore, set up his portable observatory, and install his astronomical clock and other instruments. The astronomer's main task was to take observations to check the going of the watches and to find the latitude and longitude of the place by as many different methods as possible. He also made magnetic, meteorological and tidal observations.

On the First Voyage, Cook and his brilliant astronomer, Green, had a portable observatory with wooden walls and a canvas roof, designed by John Smeaton, F.R.S., the famous civil engineer who designed the third Eddystone lighthouse. On the Second and Third Voyages the observatories (designed by William Bayly, one of the astronomers embarked) had canvas walls similar to the tent exhibited here; a contemporary engraving is shown alongside.

When an observation was to be taken, the roof could be raised off the eaves of the tent (by means of the tripod shown in the engraving), and turned round until the opening in the roof was facing the sun or whatever body was to be observed. Courtesy Sydney Parker.

Except for the three poles WZ, WX, and WY (see engraving), the whole tent could be taken down and packed in a chest 6' long by 1' 8" square. Courtesy NMG.

Source: W. Wales, *The Original Astronomical Observations made in . . . the RESOLUTION and ADVENTURE . . . 1772-5* (London, 1777), p. viii.

118. THE NAUTICAL ALMANAC FOR *1777*
Edited by Nevil Maskelyne, Astronomer Royal and a Commissioner of Longitude. NMG.

First published in 1767 (and still going strong after 200 years), the *Nautical Almanac*, and the Requisite Tables which were used with it, greatly reduced the labor of calculating the longitude at sea when the navigator was using the method of lunar distances. In his three voyages, Cook and his officers gave this new publication the best possible trial.

The *Almanac* is open to show predictions for every three hours of the angular distances from the moon ( ) to the sun ( ) and selected stars.

58

127.

Cook's opinion of this book on the First Voyage was: "Would Sea officers once apply themselves to the makeing and calculating these (lunar) observations they would not find them so very difficult as they at first imagine, especially with the assistance of the Nautical Almanac and Astronomical Ephemeris, by the help of which the calculations for finding the Long'de, takes up but little more time than that of an Azimuth for find(ing) the Vari'n of the compass." Cook's Journal, August 23rd, 1770.

119. PSALMS AND SACRED SONGS IN MANUSCRIPT
NLA, Canberra, Australia.

This small volume is said to have been written out and bound by an unknown seaman on board *Resolution* on Cook's Third Voyage.

120. MANUSCRIPT ACCOUNT BY JAMES WILES, OF THE DEATH OF PAPPO, *1793*
APL, Auckland, N.Z.

Pappo was a Tahitian who sailed in *Bounty* after the mutiny and, in 1793, in *Providence* under Captain Bligh. Wiles, a botanist, was recommended to Bligh by Banks. He sailed with Bligh on his forever memorable longboat voyage when they were cast adrift by *Bounty's* mutineers.

121. MANUSCRIPT LETTER OF 18 JANUARY 1780 TO SIR JOSEPH BANKS FROM SIR JAMES HARRIS, ST. PETERSBURG, RUSSIA
APL, Auckland, N.Z. 3 pp.

Harris expresses regret at Cook's death and refers to the appearance of Cook's ships in Russian waters, at Kamchatka on the Siberian coast. It was at this time that the Russian owned pieces were given to Commandant von Behm who served on the Peninsula in the 1770s, with headquarters at Bolsheretsk.

122. MANUSCRIPT LETTER, DATED AT MARYLEBONE (IN LONDON) 4 JANUARY 1780, TO SIR JOSEPH BANKS FROM J. NEWMAN, ENGLISH SECRETARY TO THE RUSSIAN EMBASSY IN LONDON, *APL, Auckland, N.Z. 3 pp.*

The significance of this letter lies in its two enclosures, apparently transcripts in the hand of Newman from two notes dated at St. Petersburg, 19 and 22 November 1779, relating to Cook's ships under Captains Gore and King anchoring in Petropavlovsk harbor, Kamchatka, on the Siberian coast.

(The name Petropavlovsk—St. Peter and St. Paul in English —derives from the ship names of the famous Danish Russian explorer Vitus Bering, 40 years earlier.)

123. MANUSCRIPT LETTER, OF 23 JUNE 1779, FROM

JEAN HYACINTHE DE MAGALHAENS TO SIR JOSEPH BANKS, SOHO SQUARE (LONDON)
APL, Auckland, N.Z. 2 pp.

Introduces and quotes an extract from a letter of 18 June 1779, from the Duc de Croy, Governor of Calais, concerning the latter's efforts to ensure Cook protection from French and American privateers. Although France and Spain and the rebel American colonies were all at war with Britain, all three countries instructed their navies that Cook was to "be treated as a commander of a neutral and allied power." No other explorer has ever been accorded such unique international protection, by his country's enemies, in time of war.

Dr. Benjamin Franklin, who helped correct Jefferson's first draft of the Declaration of Independence in 1776, became American envoy to Paris. He had power to issue letters of Marque against the British, but he inserted instructions to privateers that Cook was "to be shown every respect and be permitted to pass unattacked on account of the benefits he had conferred on mankind through his important discoveries."

124. COOK TO JONATHAN HARRISON, ESQ.,
Attorney at Law. Original manuscript letter dated London, February 24, 1776. NLA, Canberra.

125. ELEGY ON CAPTAIN COOK TO WHICH IS ADDED AN ODE TO THE SUN
Anna Seward, London, 1780. ATL, Wellington, N.Z.

There is no indication that Miss Seward read her Elegy before any royal body. However, the triumph experienced by Grey's elegiac country churchyard verses may account for the 2nd edition in 1780.

126. ELOGY OF CAPTAIN JAMES COOK, *1785*
Michelangiolo Gianetti, Florence, ATL, Wellington, New Zealand.

The writer composed and then recited this lengthy eulogy before the Royal Academy, Florence, on 9 June 1785.

127. JOHN WEBBER, *Artist, 1752-93*
"The peoples, seas and landscapes of all the oceans of the world came under his brush." 16½" x 13½". NMG.

Born in London he received his art training in Berne from J. L. Aberli, a German painter and engraver of picturesque views. Sent to Paris to complete his training Webber studied there and in 1775 at the Royal Academy, London.

In 1776 Dr. Solander noticed a portrait by Webber. It is said that this led to his appointment as official artist to the Third Voyage that, in Cook's words, "we might go out with every

129.

131.

help that could serve to make the result of our voyage entertaining to the generality of our readers as well as instructive to the sailor and scholar . . ."

Webber, more than any of the artists of the previous voyages, was to act as a strong visual recorder pictorializing memorable events and as an illustrator of detail to supply "the unavoidable imperfections of written accounts," as Cook put it.

Webber's paintings, therefore, lack the originality and vigor of Hodges', and his use of color is more predictable. Webber's insistence upon botanical detail often spoiled the composition of his work.

Nevertheless, the "great Variety of Portraits of Persons, Views of Places, and Historical Representations of Remarkable Incidents, drawn by Mr. Webber during the Voyage, and engraved by the most eminent artists" (as the title page of the official account of the voyage described them when it came out in 1784) became one of the main founts of the European vision of the Pacific for the next 50 years.

Furthermore, between 1788 and 1792 Webber published a series of 16 plates of Pacific views, etched and colored by himself and, in 1809 Boydell published a folio volume of these as *Views in the South Seas:* the title page bears the date 1808, but all the aquatints are dated 1809; Boydell reissued it with the same title page about 1820.

128. "CAPTAIN CHARLES CLERKE, R.N. (1743-79)," 1776
Portrait in oils by Sir Nathaniel Dance-Holland, R.A., M.P.
29½" x 24½" i.d. Government House, Wellington, His
Excellency, the Governor-General of New Zealand.

It is interesting that the exotic Maori figure in the background has been based by Dance on one of Parkinson's drawings made on the First Voyage. Clerke, an Essex farmer's son, a good seaman whose "open disposition made his company universally caressed," became one of Cook's few close friends. He had sailed on the First Voyage as Master's Mate, and was then promoted to be Third Lieutenant in *Endeavour;* on the Second Voyage as Second Lieutenant in *Resolution;* on the Third Voyage as Commander of *Discovery.* Although seriously ill he succeeded to command of *Resolution* and the expedition on Cook's death, but died of tuberculosis off Petropavlovsk on 27 August that year. Captain Gore then took the two ships back to England, with Captain King as second-in-command.

Dance was a fashionable portraitist in London. He made a large fortune as an artist and then married "an immensely wealthy widow," adding her name to his own, to become Dance-Holland. He then took up politics and entered Parliament, but is best known for his universally popular portrait of Cook in the National Maritime Museum. This portrait of

Clerke belonged to Admiral Isaac Smith, Mrs. Cook's cousin who sailed in *Endeavour* as a youth and was the first white man to set foot in New South Wales, Australia. (See his snuff-box on exhibit.) When his effects were sold in 1831 it was bought by the 5th Viscount Galway. In 1941 this striking portrait was presented to Government House by his great-grandson the late 8th Viscount Galway, GCMG, DSO, OBE, Governor-General and Commander-in-Chief of New Zealand (1935-41). He also gave the figurehead of *Resolution* (on exhibit) to the National Museum of New Zealand.

129. CAPTAIN JOHN GORE, R.N. (*ca 1730-90*)
By John Webber, R.A. (1752-93). Oil painting on canvas, 1780.
NLA, Canberra, Australia from the Rex Nan Kivell Collection.

Gore was an American, believed to have been born in Virginia. He joined the Royal Navy in 1755 and served in the Seven Years' War as a midshipman. He sailed round the world twice as Master's Mate in HMS *Dolphin*, the first time under the Hon. John Byron, the second time under Captain Samuel Wallis, with another mate, Robert Molyneux. He was Third Lieutenant under Cook in *Endeavour* on the First Voyage, being promoted Second Lieutenant on the death of Hicks. Gore missed the Second Voyage, having been given leave to travel to Iceland as a guest of Banks.

On the Third Voyage he began as First Lieutenant in *Resolution* under Cook, but after the latter's death Captain Clerke transferred to that vessel and appointed the durable Gore as Captain of *Discovery* in his place. When Clerke died, Gore took command of the expedition and brought it safely home to England, where he was promoted to the rank of Post-Captain. On his death he was praised as "A most experienced seaman and an honour to his profession." Among the several Americans in Cook's expeditions, the hardy Gore obviously possessed all the skills of a master mariner, but not the instincts of an explorer.

130. CAPTAIN JAMES KING, R.N., F.R.S. (1750-84)
By John Webber, R.A. Oil painting on canvas. 12½" x 10".
NLA, Canberra, from the Rex Nan Kivell Collection.

King was well-born, with naval, ecclesiastical, and political connections, the son of a clergyman in the north of England. Like Cook, he served under Palliser on the Newfoundland Station and then in the Mediterranean. King attained his lieutenancy in 1771, but in 1774 left the Navy for some years to study science first in Paris, then at Oxford University.

King was commissioned as Second Lieutenant in *Resolution* but was promoted by Clerke, after Cook's death, to become First Lieutenant in *Discovery.* When Clerke died, Gore appointed King to succeed him as Captain of *Discovery* for the

132. 133.

134.

long voyage from Kamchatka to England. On his return King was promoted to Post-Captain, and in 1782 his brilliance was recognized by an election as a Fellow of the Royal Society. It was he who wrote the third volume (covering events after Cook's death) of the official account of the Third Voyage. In ill health, he retired to the French Riviera in 1783, where he died of tuberculosis in Nice the following year.

131. CAPTAIN JAMES KING, R.N. (1750-84)
Engraving by I. Hogg after S. Shelley. 12½" x 10". NMG.

132. WILLIAM BLIGH
Drawing by George Dance, NPL, London.

George Dance would surely have done his best by the notorious Captain Bligh in this profile study, taken probably in preparation for an official portrait of the already severally-plagued British naval Captain.

There is no doubt he was an extraordinarily capable seaman and, at first, a lucky one. Imagine being taken as a 21-year-old ship master to operate *Resolution* under the great navigator. And yet it is true there was a terrible personality flaw. He should always have sailed alone.

133. MIDSHIPMAN JAMES WARD (ca 1758-1801)
Oil painting by an unidentified artist, ca 1780. 30" x 25". NMG, London.

He was said to be the first man to sight the Hawaiian Group on 18 January 1778. When Cook was killed on the beach at Kealakekua Bay in February, 1779, Ward was on shore within a few feet of him but escaped on one of the boats. Ward was 18 years old when he joined *Resolution* from the Royal Academy, Portsmouth, on 19 February 1776 as an Able Seaman. He was rated Midshipman on 2 November 1779, and Lieutenant in August, 1782, nearly two years after the ships' return. He served in the East India Station 1782-84.

134. "A VIEW OF CHRISTMAS HARBOUR IN KERGUELEN'S LAND," 1776
By John Webber, R.A. (1752-93), DL, LNSW, Sydney, Australia. 22.3 x 42 cm. Watercolor.

Another wash drawing of this same picture, by Webber, is in the British Museum; and an engraving by J. Newton is Pl. IV in the official account of the Third Voyage.

Kerguelen Island, largest in the southern Indian Ocean, discovered in 1772 by the Frenchman whose name it bears, was visited by Cook in December, 1776. After sailing through fogs so thick that the ships kept in touch only by the repeated firing of their guns, he found it "naked and disolate in the highest degree." Of the penguins so prominent in the fore-

ground, William Bayly, the astronomer, wrote that there were "Penguins Innumerable which were not bad eating when properly managed in Cooking."

The ships anchored on 25 December in Christmas Harbor, hence Cook's naming of it; but it is now again known as Baie de l'Oiseau, as Kerguelen called it on his second visit of 1776, of which Cook was unaware. He noted that because the men had been kept so busy the day they arrived at this Island of Desolation, Christmas was not celebrated until 27 December —and spartan it was, then.

135. THE ISLAND OF DESOLATION, 1776
View of Christmas Harbor, in Kerguelen's Land. An original watercolor and engraving by Newton after J. Webber (1752-93). 18½" x 23½". NMG.

On his way out on the Second Voyage Cook had learned at the Cape of Good Hope that Yves de Kerguelen had reported sighting land in latitude 48° S. and in the longitude of Mauritius (he was some 20° of longitude in error). Cook had searched for it on his first Antarctic sweep and missed it by some 10°. Now, on leaving the Cape on the outward leg of his Third Voyage, he ran down the latitude of Kerguelen Island until he sighted it on 24 December, 1776, in latitude 48½° S., longitude 68° 40' E.

So bare was it of vegetation that he called it the Island of Desolation.

Tues. 24 (December, 1776) ". . . we made sure of finding a good harbour . . . I immediately dispatched Mr. Bligh the Master in a boat to sound the Harbour, who on his return reported it to be safe and commodious . . . and great plenty of fresh Water, Seals, Penguins and other birds on the shore but not a stick of wood . . . so fearless that we killed as ma(ny) as we chose for the sake of their fat or blubber to make Oil for our lamps . . ."

Thanks to the accuracy of Cook's position the seals were soon exterminated by sealers.

Engraving from J. Cook and King (1784), Pl. 4. The original wash drawing is British Museum Add. MS. 15513.3.

136. VIEW OF SHIP COVE, QUEEN CHARLOTTE SOUND, NEW ZEALAND, FEBRUARY, 1777
In oil on canvas by John Webber, R.A. 23" x 30". BSG, Nelson, N.Z.

The title on the frame is wrong—Cook's Cove is in Tolaga Bay in the North Island, visited on the First Voyage, but never seen by Webber. Cook wrote in his journal, on his fourth and last visit in February, 1777: "On the 13th set up the observatory . . . erected two tents upon the same spot we formerly had them . . . two men were appointed to brew spruce beer" as an antiscorbutic remedy, and to conserve supplies of grog. Web-

THE POA.

ber painted this oil in 1778 from earlier drawings, and he exhibited it at the Royal Academy in 1789, entitled "View of Queen Charlotte's Sound, New Zealand." In 1790 he made an aquatint of it with the same title, and it was reproduced again in the posthumous volume of aquatints, *Views in the South Seas,* published in 1809. It was at Ship Cove that Sir Joseph Banks wrote in his journal of the First Voyage: "17 January 1770—This morn I was awaked by the singing of birds ashore from whence we are distant not a quarter of a mile . . . the most melodious wild musick I have ever heard, almost imitating small bells but with the most tuneable silver sound imaginable . . ." It was in a nearby cove that a boat's crew from *Adventure* was killed and eaten on the Second Voyage.

This painting was presented to the Nelson gallery in 1931 by the late Sir Francis Dillon Bell.

137. "THE POA. FROM THE BIRD WHICH WAS BROUGHT BACK FROM NEW ZEELAND BY CAPT. COOK, IN HIS LATE VOYAGE ROUND THE WORLD AND WHICH OBTAINED OF THE SOCIETY OF ARTS A PREMIUM OF 30 GUINEAS. R. LAURIE, DEL. ET FECt,"

Sir Alister McIntosh, KCMG, Wellington, N.Z.
Mezzotint in color. 16" x 12½" i.d.

The bird (*Prosthemadera novaeseelandiae*) is known by its Maori name of *tui.* Early settlers called it the Parson-bird, because of its white throat-feathers, which also caused Cook to name it the "poy-bird" as he explains May 1773 in his published account of the Second Voyage: "The feathers of a fine mazarine blue, except those of its neck, which are of a most beautiful silver-grey, and two or three short white ones, which are on the pinion joint of the wing. Under its throat hang two little tufts of curled, snow-white feathers, called its *poies,* which being the Otaheitean word for ear-rings, occasioned our giving that name to the bird; which is not more remarkable for the beauty of its plumage than for the sweetness of its note. The flesh is also most delicious, and was the greatest luxury the woods afforded us."

The name was rendered variously as Poe, Poy, and Poa, and Pl. lii in the 1777 official account of the Second Voyage is entitled "Poe-Bird, New Zealand." It is after a painting by George Forster, preserved in the Banks collection of bird paintings in the British Museum (Natural History), but lacks the natural grace and beauty of the bird as achieved by Laurie. The first illustration of a *tui* was published in 1776 in Peter Brown's *Nouvelles Illustrations de Zoologie* (London). Brown, like Laurie, worked from the stuffed specimen taken back to England.

Laurie's print (also 1776) is the first colored representation

published, and it is excessively rare. Although there might be others in existence, the Alexander Turnbull Library, in collaboration with Mr. and Mrs. D. G. Ellis of Christchurch, New Zealand, traced only nine examples, in England, Australia, and New Zealand. There are variants in these, one lacking any coloring and another, in the Mitchell Library, Sydney, being a later hand-colored engraving published in London by J. Sharpe, 1786. Robert Laurie had invented a new process of printing mezzotints in color, and it was for this that he received the Society of Arts award of 30 guineas. It seems likely that all the "Poa" prints known were proof specimens and that the work was never actually released for publication. Two of the three in New Zealand are in private hands, including this fine example purchased in London by Sir Alister in 1948.

138. TEMPORARY HABITATIONS OF THE MAORIS, 1777

Pen-and-wash tinted drawing, signed John Webber del 1777.
21" x 27". NMG, London.

From the Cape of Good Hope, after identifying the recent French discoveries to the southeastward, Cook had left Kerguelen Island on 30 December 1776, for his base in New Zealand, sailing by way of Tasmania. He anchored in Queen Charlotte's Sound, New Zealand, on 12 February 1777.

The next day, he set up the observatory and "during the course of the day a great many Families came from different parts and took up their residence by us, so that there was not a place in the Cove where a Hut could be built that was not occupied by some or another."

Cook described the building of these settlements, how the men put up the huts while the women secured the canoes, collected provisions and gathered firewood, adding: "Mr. Webber has made a drawing of one of these Villages that will convey a better idea of them than any written description." Cook, Journal.

Webber had the odd artistic convention of the time of greatly elongating the trunk of human figures and this is particularly noticeable in this drawing. Courtesy, NMG.

138a. PORTRAIT OF A NEW ZEALANDER

By John Webber. Pen and wash tinted drawing.
LNSW, Sydney, Australia.

"The Natives of this Country are a strong raw boned well made Active people rather above . . . the common size . . . They are all of a very dark brown Colour with black hair, thin black beards and white teeth . . . The men generally wear their hair long combed up and tied upon the crown . . . They seem to enjoy a good state of health and many of them live to a good old age." Cook (1770) Journal, 278-79.

THE DEATH OF CAPTAIN COOK
Aquatint by F. Jukes from John Cleveley. See Cat. no. 178.

Cook also commented in full on their tattooing, their general bravery, and the number of slain enemies they ate.

139. "VIEW OF DISCOVERY ISLAND (MANGAIA, COOK ISLANDS), MARCH 1777"
Watercolor drawing by William W. Ellis (d 1785). Signed and dated 1779. HL, Dunedin, N.Z.

On 29 March 1777 Cook discovered the islands bearing his name while en route from New Zealand to Tahiti. The Cook Islands and Cook Strait in New Zealand are the only two major features he named after himself. He landed first at the island of Mangaia, now known by this native name rather than as Discovery Island, so called by Cook for his ship. Since Ellis dated this picture 1779, he must have made a later watercolor drawing from a preliminary sketch taken in 1777 at Mangaia. The painting was purchased in 1904 by the Hocken Library from Mr. K. A. Webster, a New Zealand-born art dealer in London.

140. THE ANCHORAGE AT NUKUALOFA, TONGA, *1777*
RESOLUTION and DISCOVERY at Tongatapu, Friendly Islands. Aquatint by F. Jukes from John Cleveley after James Cleveley, fl 1780. 26" x 31¾". NMG.

After leaving New Zealand, Cook renewed his exploration of the Friendly Islands spending a month at this anchorage replenishing his water and food supplies, and repairing rigging. The sailmaker can be seen at work in the foreground.

Wed. 11 (June 1777). "I had the sails a shore to repair and a party cuting wood for fuel and Plank for the use of the Ship. The gunners of both Ships were ordered a shore to traffick with the natives, who thronged from all parts with Hogs, yams, & cocoanuts & ca. so that our little port was like a fair . . ."

On July 5th the scientists with Cook observed an eclipse of the sun from on shore. Conditions were not ideal and Cook records: ". . . the Weather was dark and cloudy . . . within a Minute or two of the beginning of the Eclipse. Everyone was at their Telescopes viz Mr. Bayly, Mr. King, Captain Clerke, Mr. Bligh and myself. I lost the observation by not having a dark glass at hand . . . Mr. Bligh had not got the Sun in the field of his Telescope, so that it was only observed by the other three." Cook, Journal.

141. A NIGHT DANCE BY WOMEN, IN HAPAEE (HA'APAI) *1777*
Engraving by Wm. Sharp after J. Webber. 18½" x 23½". NMG, London.

Cook spent six days anchored off Lifuka in the Friendly Islands (Tonga) and during this time both the islanders and the Europeans attempted to outshine each other with entertainments.

Sunday 18th (May, 1777) "A number of men seated themselves in a circle before us and began a song . . . the musick was in the middle of the circle and consisted simply of two large pieces of bamboo with which they struck the ground endways and produced a hollow dead sound . . . In a short time a number of Women . . . came and encircled the men in a kind of dance and joined in the song." Cook, Journal.

Engraving from Cook and King (1784), Pl. 17.

142. A NIGHT DANCE BY MEN, IN (HA'APAI)
Engraved by Wm. Sharp after J. Webber. 18½" x 23½". NMG.

Sunday 18th (May, 1777) "Both men and women accompanied the Song with a variety of motions of the hands and snaping of the fingers, which seems to be an essential part of their singing; their voices are however extremely musical and their actions graceful . . ."

Cook, Journal. Cook and King (1784), Pl. 16.

143. ASTRONOMICAL OBSERVATIONS AT ANAMOOKA, *1777*. "A View at Anamooka."
Engraving by W. Burne after J. Webber. 18¼" x 28¼". NMG.

Cook anchored at his old anchorage on the north side of the island, in the Tongan group, to replenish his water supply. Captain Clerke of *Discovery* and other officers went ashore to find an observatory site, and Bayly commented: ". . . Went on shore to look for a convenient place to observe in where I met Capt. Cook who objected to my going on shore with my Insts on account of the insufficiency of the Guard . . . he proposed my going on Shore with my Astronomical Quadrant only."

Bayly can be seen observing with his quadrant, mounted on a cask filled with wet sand, by the nearest palm tree. Courtesy, NMG.

144. "HUT AND THREE NATIVES OF TONGA, *1777*
By John Webber, R.A. (1752-93), DL, LNSW, Sydney, Australia. 31.2 x 45.9 cm.

Webber must have completed a 1777 rough sketch in the following year, for the expedition was at the Tongan group— Cook's Friendly Isles, first visited by him in June 1776 when he planted pineapples there—from the last days of April until the end of July, 1777.

Cook wrote of Tongan clothing and houses: "Their clothing consists of cloth, or Matting, but mostly the former, the dress of both men and Women is the same, and consists of one piece about two yards wide and two and a half long, or so long

as to go once and a half round the waist, to which it is confined by a girdle or cord; it is double before and hangs down like a petticoat as low as the middle of the leg. The upper part of the garment above the girdle is plaited into several large folds, so that there is cloth sufficient when unfolded to come over the head but this is very seldom done . . . large pieces of Cloth and fine Matting are only wore by the superior people, the inferior sort put up with some pieces and very often wear nothing but a petticoat made of the leaves of plants, or the Maro (*malo*) which is a narrow piece of cloth or matting like a Sash, this they bring between the legs and wrap round the waist; but this last is chiefly confined to the men . . . The Houses of these people are of various sizes and like those of Otaheite consists chiefly of a thatched roof supported by pillars and rafters desposed in a very judicious manner and the workman ship in many extremely neat, the floor is raised with earth smoothed and covered with strong thick Matting and kept very clean; they seldom eat in them, unless it rains . . . if the family is large they have small huts without to which they retire to sleep, so that privacy is as much observed here as one can expect."

145. "THE BODY OF TEE, A CHIEF AS PRESERVED AFTER DEATH, IN OTAHEITE," *August, 1777*
By John Webber. 31.2 x 49.7 cm. Watercolor. DL, LNSW, Sydney, Australia.

This was reproduced with the above title as Pl. 26 in the official account of the Third Voyage, engraved by W. Byrne, in reverse, with the addition of a figure in the foreground and some attention of detail. There is another Webber watercolor of the scene in the British Museum. In the Dixson Galleries of the Library of New South Wales is a third, signed by Webber, entitled on the back in an unknown hand as "A Chief lying in state, Matavi, Otaheite." Webber published his own aquatint of it on 1 July 1789, as "Waheiduoa (Vehiatua), Chief of Oheitepeha (Vaitepiha) lying in State" and this was again published in the 1809 volume of Webber aquatints as Pl. 6.

There is a good deal of confusion as to the precise identity of the corpse, as Cook gives two different accounts as below: and Beaglehole gives the name of the chief in the painting exhibited as Vehiatua, adding: "He may be identified with Tiiparii, a chief of Haapape; he is certainly not the same man as Tii-torea, the stepfather of Vehiatua" (which was a not uncommon name). And Vaitepiha Bay is some distance from Matavai Bay.

Cook's Journal, 19 August 1777 at Vaitepiha: ". . . it proved to be a Tupapow in which the remains of the late Waheiduoa [Vehiatua] laid as it were in state. . . ." The Tupapow "was covered and hung around with different Coloured cloth and Mats, so as to have a pretty effect; there was one piece of

scarlet broad Cloth of 4 or 5 Yards in length which had been given them by the Spaniards. This cloth and a few Tassels of feathers which our gentlemen took for silk made them believe it was."

Cook's Journal, 10 September 1777, at Matavai: "But the chief thing that carried me to Oparre [Pare, near Matavai] was to see an Embalmed corpse, which some of our gentlemen had met with at that place." This man (whom Cook had seen on his previous voyage) "had been dead above four months, and the body was so effectually preserved from putrefaction that there was not the least disagreeable smell about it. How this was perfirmed I could not learn any more than what Omai told me, he said they mad use of the juice of a plant which grows in the Mountains, Cocoanut Oile, and frequent washings in the Sea."

146. "A BOAT OF THE ISLAND OTAHEITA"
(Tahiti), August-December, 1777
Watercolor drawing by John Webber, R.A. HL, Dunedin, N.Z.

Tahiti—Otaheite to Cook—was named King George the Third's Island by Captain Samuel Wallis in HMS *Dolphin* when he discovered it in 1767 on his voyage around the world. Cook first arrived there in *Endeavour* on 13 April 1769, and named the group the Society Islands, "as they lie contiguous to each other." He was not, as often supposed, honoring the Royal Society which had instigated his First Voyage to record the transit of Venus.

Cook was to return to Tahiti twice more on the Second Voyage and finally for some four months on the Third Voyage, when Webber made his sketch. The drawing was acquired by the late Dr. Thomas Morland Hocken in the early years of this century.

147. A SAILING CANOE OF OTAHAITE (TAHITI)
Aquatint after J. Webber (1752-93). From J. Webber, VIEWS IN THE SOUTH SEAS (London, 1808), Pl. 3. Published April, 1809 by Boydell et Compy. 21" x 25". NMG, London.

"I went on board one of them when under sail, and by several trials with the log, found that she went seven knots, or miles in an hour close hauled, in a gentle gale . . . In these navigations, the sun is their guide by day, and the stars by night; when these are obscured, they have recourse to the points from whence the winds and the waves come upon the vessel. If during the observation, both the wind and the waves should shift . . . they are then bewildered, frequently miss their intended port, and are never heard of more." Cook, Journal, 14th August, 1770. Webber himself engraved and published the original aquatint, August, 1792.

148. VIEW IN ULIIETEA (RAIATEA, IN THE

152.

TAHITIAN ISLANDS) *1777*
By John Webber, R.A. (1752-93). Oil painting on canvas.
NLA, Canberra from the Rex Nan Kivell Collection.

Cook visited Raiatea, one of the larger of the Society Islands, on all three voyages, retaining throughout its native name as best he could interpret it. On the Third Voyage he was there from 3 November-4 December 1777. Webber could have painted this picture at the Admiralty after his return to London in 1780.

In August, 1769 Cook wrote: "Ulietea and Otaha (Tahaa) lay close to each other and are both inclosed within a reef of Coral rocks, and altho the distance between the one and the other is near 2 Miles yet their is no passage for Shipping. By means of this reef are form'd several excellent Harbours, the entrances into them are but narrow but when a ship is once in nothing can hurt her . . ."

149. VAITEPIHA BAY, TAHITI, *1777*
A View in Oteitepeha Bay, in the Island of Otaheite, J. Webber, published April 1, 1809 by Boydell & Company. From Webber, VIEWS IN THE SOUTH SEAS (London, 1808), Pl. 5. 21" x 25". NMG, London.

Cook first visited Vaitepiha Bay in 1769 and again in 1773 and 1774 on his Second Voyage. John Webber, the official artist with him on the Third Voyage drew the original of this aquatint (British Museum, Add MS 15513.13), on his last visit in August, 1777, and engraved and published it himself August 1, 1791.

It is a good example of how the beauties of Tahiti were brought before the eyes of a wider public than could see the original drawings and paintings by the official artists such as Hodges and Webber.

150. A SAFE HARBOR FOR *RESOLUTION* AND *DISCOVERY* IN THE TAHITIAN ISLANDS, *1777*
View of Moorea or Eimeo, one of the Society Islands in the South Seas. Aquatint by F. Jukes from John Cleveley (1747-86) after James Cleveley (fl 1780). 26½" x 32½". NMG, London.

Tuesday 30th (September, 1777) ". . . we stood in with the Ships and anchored close up to the head of it in 10 fathoms water over a bottom of soft mud and Moored with a hawser fast to the shore. This harbour . . . extends in south or SBE between the hills above two miles, for security and the goodness of its bottom it is not inferior to any harbour I have met with in any of the islands . . ." Cook, Journal.

It was during this stay at Moorea that Cook went to a lot of trouble to retrieve a stolen goat. After repeated threats and eventually the burning of huts and canoes the goat was returned.

Cook's unusual ruthlessness caused many of his companions to comment on such harshness. From one who was generally very understanding in his treatment of the natives, it was, perhaps, a sign of the accumulated effects of the prolonged strain which Cook had undergone in the course of three voyages into the remotest parts of the world. Eventually it was to result in the fatal error of judgment at Hawaii which was to provoke the natives into sudden violence ending in his death, 1779.

151. A BARBAROUS CUSTOM
A Human Sacrifice, in a Morai, in Otaheite, 1777. Engraving by W. Woollett after J. Webber (1752-93). 19" x 26½". NMG, London.

Cook had visited Tahiti in 1769, 1773 and 1774. This was his fourth and also his last visit. The chiefs were becoming familiar with him and talked more frankly. They now invited him to watch a human sacrifice—that of a middle-aged criminal of the lowest class who had been clubbed to death the day before. This sacrifice was made to invoke success for an expedition against the neighbouring island of Moorea.

Mon. 1 September (1777) "I thought this a good opportunity to see something of this extraordinary and Barbarous custom . . ." Cook, Journal.

Cook and King, 1784, Pl. 25.

152. THE PLOT THAT FAILED, AT RAIATEA, TAHITIAN ISLANDS, *1777*
Watercolor by J. Webber (1752-93). 21¾" x 27". NMG, London.

Webber, unlike Hodges, did not experiment with his art. This watercolor is typical of his style, and was exhibited at the Royal Academy in 1787. He attempted to render tropical light and color by "tinted" color; this tended to paleness or a stained effect alien to the brilliance of the actual scene. However, watercolor painting was still in its early stages of development.

The outrigger canoe is typical of those that lay around the ship at Raiatea when, on Wednesday, November 26, 1777, "Between five and six of Clock in the evening all the Indians that were in and about the harbour and ships began to move off, as if some sudden panick had seized them . . . they called to us from the *Discovery* . . . that a party of Indians had seized Captain Clerke and Mr. Gore who had walked out a little way from the ships. . . . It was evedent . . . the next day . . . their first and great design was to have got me. It was my custom to go and bathe in the fresh Water every evening and very often alone and always without arms . . ." Cook, Journal. Courtesy, NMG.

155.

157.

153. POETUA, "PRINCESS" OF RAIATEA ON THE SOCIETY ISLANDS, DAUGHTER OF OREO, *November, 1777*
By John Webber. Oil painting on canvas. NLA, Canberra, Australia from the Rex Nan Kivell Collection.

"Queens have died young and fair," quoted Beaglehole in an unusual expression of sentiment when writing of the beautiful Poetua, called Po-dua, Poeeddah, and Poldowi by Cook and his men. Australian Professor Bernard Smith wrote of this South Seas Mona Lisa: the "highly romantic image of a firm-breasted young Raiatean girl bare to the waist, who wears the flowers of Cape jasmin in her hair and a Giaconda look upon her face."

Poetua was involved in an incident that was happily resolved although it could have had unfortunate consequences. Two men from *Discovery*, Alexander Mouat, a midshipman, and Thomas Shaw, a gunner's mate, deserted—"the engaging females were the inducement." When Cook learned that the Raiateans apparently intended to conceal them, he had Clerke seize Oreo's daughter, her husband, and the Chief's son, holding them hostage until the two men were returned. Oreo then plotted to seize Cook when he went ashore to bathe in fresh water, as he did "every evening and very often alone and without arms." Cook, however, had already realized the danger of such a possibility and refrained from his usual bath, cautioning Clerke and the other officers to take no risks. Three days later Oreo's men captured the deserters on the adjacent island of Borabora and returned them, whereupon the involuntary guests were released from *Discovery*.

Webber painted his portrait of Poetua at the Admiralty after he returned to London in 1780; there is one such painting at the National Maritime Museum, Greenwich, and this second painting in Canberra, entitled "Poedowi, daughter of Urei."

154. A VIEW OF HUAHEINE, *1777*
Engraving by W. Byrne after J. Webber. 18" x 26½". NMG.

Sunday 12th (October, 1777) ". . . at Noon we Anchored at the North entrance of O Wharre (Fare) harbour which is on the West side of the island . . . I set up a tent a shore, established a post, there set up the observatory to make the necessary Observations and the Carpenters . . . were set to work to build a small house for Omai to secure his property in . . ." Cook, Journal.

The observatory tents can just be seen close to the shore on the far side of the bay, with Omai's small house to the left of them and in front of the chiefs' assembly house.

Cook landed Omai at this island, with his remaining European possessions, and gave him a musket, fowling piece, pistol and ammunition. Omai being of humble birth had aroused

the jealousies of the princes in Tahiti by his European wealth and foolish lavishness when he was landed there. With him were left two New Zealand youths whom Cook had been persuaded to take from Queen Charlotte Sound in February, 1777, as companions to Omai.

Bligh enquired after them all when *Bounty* was brought to in the bay in April, 1789. It was learned all had died natural deaths, some two-and-a-half to four years after Cook left them.

Engraving from Cook and King (1786), Pl. 31.

155. VIEW OF HUAHEINE, ONE OF THE SOCIETY ISLANDS IN THE SOUTH SEAS
Aquatint by F. Jukes from John Cleveley after James Cleveley, fl 1780. (Published London 1788.) 26" x 31½". NMG.

Sunday 12th (October, 1777) ". . . I set up a tent a shore, established a post, there set up the observatory to make the necessary Observations . . ." Cook, Journal.

The objects mentioned in Cook's description of the day's activities are clearly shown in this aquatint. Notwithstanding the troubles over the stolen goat in Moorea, and the much-publicized punitive action by Cook, a sextant was stolen from Bayly's observatory. Cook's prompt action in going ashore and demanding its return and confining the thief in the *Resolution* resulted in it being found the following day.

156. A CANOE OF THE SANDWICH ISLANDS, THE ROWERS MASKED
Engraving by C. Grignion after J. Webber. 18¼" x 23¼". NMG, London.

(Mon. 2 February, 1778) ". . . they make their Canoes; as they are in general about twenty four feet long and the bottom for the most part formed of one piece, hollowed out to about an inch, or an inch and a half thick, and brought to a point at each end . . . The extremities of both head and stern is a little raised, and both are made sharp, something like a wedge . . They rowed by paddles and some have a light triangular sail . . . extended to a mast and boom." Cook, Journal.

The shape of the sail is peculiar to these islands but the craft reflect the Polynesian character of these oceanic canoes. The gourd masks were associated with worship of the god Lono; the Hawaiians believed Cook to be him.

Engraving from Cook and King (1784), Pl. 65.

157. "A SAILING CANOE OF SANDWICH ISLANDS OR OWHYEE" (Hawaii), *1778-79*
Pen and wash drawing by John Webber, R.A., HL, Dunedin, N.Z.

The varied types of canvas used in the Pacific and drawn by artists on all three voyages are now valued by research workers.

158 a.

This picture was acquired in the early part of this century by the late Dr. Thomas Moreland Hocken.

"... the Mast ... is secured by shrouds and stays. One end of the Yard rests against the foot of the Mast and taking a sweep forms an arck of a circle, the upper end of which is as high as the mast head; the Sail's made of strong Matting sewed together and is joined to the Mast and the Yard, at the upper end forms a half Moon which gives their canoes when under sail a very singular appearance; they generally have a bunch of black feathers at the mast head and at the end of the yard a kind of pendant flying made of Cloth. In the Stern of their Canoes they carry small Wooden Images which they call Etee [(h) Ki'i]. Some of the double Canoes are twenty Yards long, are strongly put together, and will answer the purpose very well of going from one Island to the (other) which probably is the Extent of the Navigation of these people. Some of the largest canoes will hold about sixty or seventy Men." Samwell's Journal.

158. "BOXING MATCH BEFORE CAPT. COOK AT OWYHEE, SANDWICH ISLANDS, THURSDAY, JANUARY 28TH, 1779"
Webber lithograph. From the collections of the Daughters of Hawaii at Hulihee Palace, Kailua-Kona, Hawaii.

From an unpublished drawing by James (i.e. John) Webber, a limited edition of 150 copies was made at the time of sale by Francis Edwards, London, 1919.

158a. BARTERING IN THE SANDWICH (HAWAIIAN) ISLANDS, 1778
An Inland View, in Atooi. Engraving by S. Middiman after J.Webber. 18" x 27½". NMG.

Friday 30th (January, 1778) "... I sent Mr. Gore ashore again with a guard of Marines and a party to trade with the Natives for refreshments: ... they returned with a few yams and salt ..." Cook, Journal.

The following day Cook went ashore with a party to fill water casks and also to indulge in more bartering at Waimea village on Kauai (Atooi). The currency used by the crew in these stone age islands is much in evidence in this print: a large iron nail and an iron axe are both being offered in exchange for island produce.

Cook was the European discoverer of the Hawaiian Islands, which form the northern apex of the Polynesian triangle.

For two centuries the Manila-Acapulco Spanish galleons had passed to the south and to the north of them and for reasons almost inexplicable seem never to have seen the islands.

Engraving from Cook and King (1786), Pl. 35.

159. A YOUNG WOMAN OF THE SANDWICH ISLANDS
Engraving by J. K. Sherwin after J. Webber (1752-93). 19½" x 16½". NMG.

William Ellis, *Discovery's* surgeon's second mate, had the following ungallant remarks about the women of the Sandwich Islands noted in his journal: "The women were rather ordinary, and in general masculine and will scarce bear a comparison with the fair dames of Taheitee ..." Talented Ellis, in spite of Clerke's dying recommendation of him to Banks' attention as a very worthy young man, was, a year after the end of the voyage, badly in need of money, and in spite of official prohibitions to publish, found a bookseller's offer of 50 guineas irresistible. He therefore published *An Authentic Narrative of a Voyage performed by Captain Cook and Captain Clerke, in His Majesty's ships Resolution and Discovery* ... 2 Volumes, London, 1782, and thereby forfeited Banks' patronage forever and ruined his naval career.

The original drawing by Webber in the British Museum (Add. MS. 1551425), is much less charming and romantic.

Engraving from Cook and King (1784), Pl. 63.

160. "A CHIEF OF THE SANDWICH (HAWAIIAN) ISLANDS," 1778-79
By John Webber, R.A. (1752-93). Oil painting on canvas. NLA, Canberra, Australia, from the Rex Nan Kivell Collection.

On 18 January 1778 Cook sighted Oahu in the Hawaiian Islands, which he named for the Earl of Sandwich, the First Lord of the Admiralty and his stout patron. Then came Kauai, and next day Niihau. The first European landing was on Kauai, on 20 January, and on Niihau on the 29th. They stayed for a fortnight before sailing on to the Oregon coast, and it was not until 26 November 1778, after arduous months in Arctic waters, that the two ships returned to the Sandwich Islands, sighting Maui to the north.

Cook described the clothing worn by the natives in an entry in his journal, February 1778: "These people are scanty in their cloathing, very few of the men wear any thing more than the Maro (or *malo*), but the women have a piece of cloth wraped round the waist so as to hang down like a petticoat as low as the knee; all the rest of the body is naked. Thier ornaments are braclets, necklaces and amulets, which are made of shells, bone or stone; They have also neat Tippets made of red and yellow feathers, and Caps and Cloaks covered with the same or some other feathers; the cloakes (*ahu-ula*) reach to about the middle of the back, and are like the short cloakes worn by the women in England, or like the riding cloaks worn in Spain. The Caps (*mahiole*) are made so as to fit very close to

164.

165.

the head with a semicircular protuberance on the crown exactly like the helmets of old. These and also the cloaks they set so high a value upon that I could not procure one, some were however got."

However, Cook later received a magnificent specimen from the royal hand.

161. FEATHER HELMETS AND CLOAKS, *1778*
A Man of the Sandwich Islands, with his Helmet.
Engravings by J. K. Sherwin after Webber (1752-93).
19½" x 16½". NMG, London.

Mon. 2 February, 1778 "They have also neat Tippets made of red and yellow feathers, and Caps and Cloaks covered with the same or some other feathers . . . The Caps are made so as to fit very close to the head with a semicircular protuberance on the crown exactly like the helmets of old . . ."Cook, Journal.

These famous feather-covered garments were worn only by chiefs and were highly valuable: made with great skill, they are oddly attractive.

In his painting "The Death of Cook," John Zoffany made the murderer a chieftain wearing just such a helmet and by this means and the constrained tension of stance combined realism with neo-classical tradition in art.

The exceedingly rare helmet seen in the Exhibition is from the Cook Collection via Behm to Catherine the Great (1780) in the Museum of Ethnography, Leningrad. [Withdrawn.]
Engraving from Cook and King (1784), Pl. 44.

162. CAPTAIN COOK SIGHTS OREGON
Cape Foulweather, Oregon Coast. Photograph, OHS Collections.

After an uneventful fine week passage a high headland was seen "which I called Cape Foulweather from the very bad weather we soon after met with." Cook had reached the Oregon coast very close to the latitude where Francis Drake had broken his northern exploration.

163. CAPE PERPETUA, OREGON COAST
Photograph, OHS Collections.

The expedition hung close to the stormy coast, accurately fixing four capes of which two retain Cook's names. Clerke entered in his log the heavy and dangerous westerly swell: ". . . we can't look at the shore, but continue to dance about in the Offing here & make the best Weather of it we can." Cook was not commemorating a saint's day, but rather the fact that Cape Perpetua seemed always in his sight.

163a. A SEA OTTER
Engraving after John Webber, photograph, OHS Collections.

Cook's three voyages were of everlasting geographical im-

portance, and his findings not only excited London but all of Europe. His reports were known everywhere and especially interesting were those that revealed something of the fisheries or other sources of economic wealth.

Hence the Third Voyage was perhaps the most exciting of all when the crew learned how desirable the carelessly worn sea otter cloaks of Nootka Sound were. When the traders among the crew reached Chinese ports they discovered that even the shabbier "sea beaver" skins were, like Russian sables, referred to as "soft gold." This is the trade that immediately opened up the North Pacific.

164. "A VIEW OF THE HABITATIONS IN NOOTKA SOUND," *April 1778*
By John Webber, R.A. (1752-93). 22.3 x 37.9 cm.
Watercolor. DL, LNSW, Sydney, Australia.

There is another drawing by Webber in the British Museum, and S. Smith engraved Pl. XLI of this view for the official account of the Third Voyage.

Cook was anchored from 30 March-26 April in Resolution Cove at the southeast end of Clerke Peninsula, projecting southward from Bligh Island in Nootka Sound, Vancouver Island. He christened the sound King George's Sound. On 22 April he visited a village "at the west point of the Sound . . . During the time I was at this village Mr. Webber who was with me made drawings of every thing that was curious both within and without doors; I had also an oppertunity to inspect more narrowly into their houses, household affairs . . ."

Clerke called it a "Town of the Natives situated in a Bay near the mouth of the Sound: we were receiv'd and treated during our Stay, with every kind of civility and attention by the Principals of this habitation; they really made most hospitable offers, but our difference in taste and idea of what is good and palatable, wou'd not permit us to avail ourselves of this part of their kindness . . ."

165. "THE INSIDE OF A HOUSE IN NOOTKA SOUND," *April, 1778*
By John Webber, R.A. (1752-93). 48.1 x 42.7 cm.
Watercolor. DL, LNSW, Sydney, Australia.

Again there is another Webber drawing, this time in the Peabody Museum, Harvard University. W. Sharp engraved Pl. XLII of this view for the official account of the Third Voyage.

Cook comments: "At the upper end of many of the appartments, were two large images, or statues placed abreast of each other and 3 or 4 feet asunder, they bore some resemblance to the human figure, but monsterous large; the best idea will be

166.

had of them in a drawing which Mr. Webber made of the inside of one of thir appartments wherein two of them stood . . . . This made some of our gentlemen think they were their gods, but I am not altogether of that opinion, at least if they were they hild them very cheap, for with a small matter of iron or brass, I could have purchased all the gods in the place, for I did not see one that was not offered me, and two or three of the very smalest sort I got."

On 31 December 1783 Webber wrote to Canon Douglas, who was editing the publication of the official account of the Third Voyage: "After having made a general view of the dwellings I sought for an inside which would furnish me with sufficient matter to convey a perfect Idea of the mode these people live in. Such was soon found . . . While I was employ'd a man approach'd me with a large knife in one hand seemingly displeas'd . . .

"Being certain of no future oppertunity to finish my Drawing & the object too interesting for leaving unfinish'd, I considered a little bribery might have some effect, and accordingly made an offer of a button from my coat, which color of metal they are much pleas'd with, this instantly produc'd the desir'd effect, for the mat was remov'd and I left at liberty to proceed as before. scarcely had I seated myself and made a beginning, but he return'd & renewd his former practice, till he'd disposed of my buttons, after which time I found no opposition in my further employment."

166. "A WOMAN OF NOOTKA SOUND" and "A MAN OF NOOTKA SOUND," *April, 1778*
By John Webber, R.A., 23.9 x 17.9 cm. and 23.2 x 17.5 cm. respectively. DL, LNSW, Sydney, Australia.

Duplicates by Webber are in the Peabody Museum of Archaeology and Ethnology, Harvard University (the Woman) and the Public Archives of Canada, Ottawa (the Man). Appears as Pl. XXXIX of the official account of the Third Voyage.

In his general account of the area and its people, Cook gave some considerable detail: "I can form no estimate of the number of Inhabitants . . . And they as also all others who visited us are, both men and Women, of a small Stature, some, Women in particular, very much so and hardly one, even of the younger sort, had the least pretentions to being call'd beauties. Their face is rather broad and flat, with highish cheek bones and plump cheeks. Their mouth is little and round, the nose neither flat nor prominent; their eyes are black little and devoid of sparkling fire. . . . they paint with a liberal hand, and are slovenly to the last degree. Their hair is black or dark brown, straight, strong, and long, in general they wear it

flowing . . . They are a docile, courtious good natured people, but very passionate and quick in resenting what they looke upon as an injury, and like most other passionate people as soon forget it . . . At other times they are commonly grave and silent and are by no means talkative people . . . Their Cloaths are made of the skins of land and Sea animals, in the making of which there is very little of either art or trouble, besides that of dressing the skins and sewing them together for they do no more than form them into a kind of Cloak which is tied over the shoulders with a string and reaches as low as the knees. . . . For a head dress they have a strong straw hat which is shaped like a flower-pot and is as good a covering for the head as can possibly be invented. Thus cloathed, with sometimes the addition of Coarse Mat over all, they sit in their Canoes in the heaviest rain as unconcerned as we can under the best of cover . . .

"Both Men and Women paint their faces, their colours are black red and white and seemed to be a kind of ochre mixed with oil . . . in this plaster they make various scrawls on the face and particularly on the fore head. Besides this daubing they have another ornament to the Face, which is a small circular plate, or flat ring in the shape of a horse shoe, but not more in circumference than a shilling; the upper part is cut asunder, so as the two points may gently pinch the Bridle of the Nose, to which it hangs over the upper lip. These ornaments were made of either iron or copper and the rims of some of our buttons were appropriated to this use."

167. VIEW IN KING GEORGE'S SOUND, N.W. COAST OF AMERICA
William Ellis. Watercolor and ink. 9″ x 10¾″ Rex Nan Kivell Collection, NLA, Canberra, Australia.

Ellis, a Cambridge graduate, was surgeon's mate on *Discovery* during the Third Voyage and acted as the natural history draftsman. He did some of the most important detail work, for which we are ever grateful. This view of the harbor we know today as Nootka is but one of his many extant drawings. Much of his work is in the British Museum (Natural History) but 29 watercolors and other drawings are in the National Library of Australia from where this and 20 others are kindly loaned.

168. VIEW IN KING GEORGE'S SOUND
William Ellis, Watercolor. 11¾″ x 17″. NLA, Canberra.

Soon to drift back to the Indian name, Nootka, this noble body of water was appropriate to so great a monarch. Yet it is unpredictable, full of shoals, pinnacles and unexpected reefs, and prey to sudden squalls and storms at any season, black and

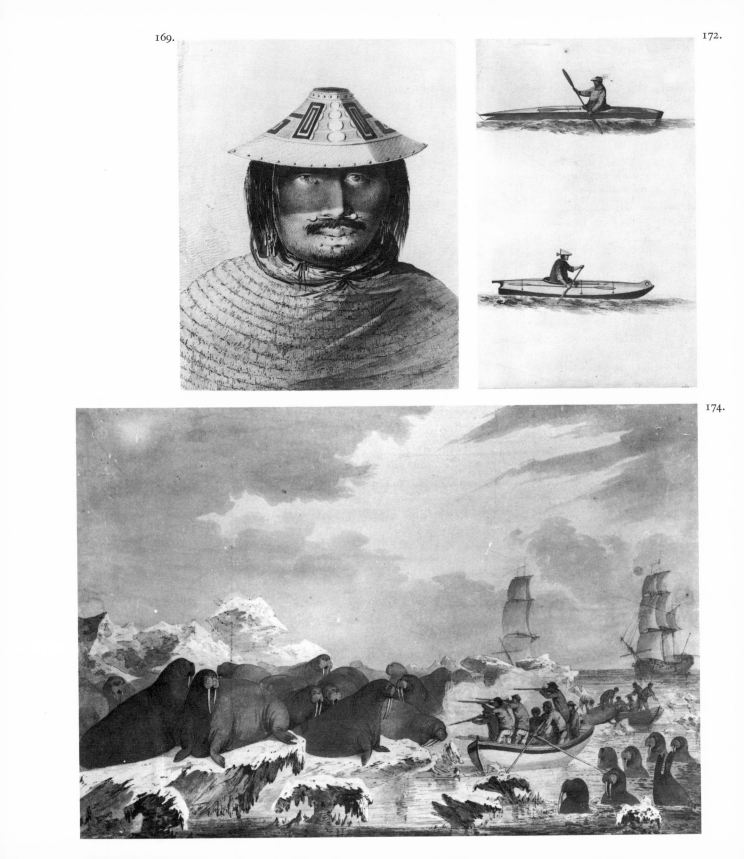

169.

172.

174.

dangerous as the Hanoverian king was in his increasingly fitful mind.

169. "A MAN OF PRINCE WILLIAM'S SOUND,"
May 1778
By John Webber, R.A. 23 x 18.2 cm. Watercolor.
DL, LNSW, Sydney, Australia.

Also in the Peabody Museum of Archaeology and Ethnology, Harvard University; engraved by J. Basire as Pl. XLVII in the official account of the Third Voyage. Cook wrote: "These people are not of the same Nation as those who Inhabit King Georges Sound, both their language and features are widely different: These are small of stature, but thick set good looking people and from Crantz description of the Greenlander, seem to bear some affinity to them. But as I never saw either a Greenlander or an Esquemaus, who are said to be of the same nation, I cannot be a sufficient judge . . ."

And Clerke: "The Natives here are fine jolly full fac'd Fellows, abounding to all appearance in good living and content: they have very chearfull countenances, and in their conversation with each other, there appears a good deal of repartee and laugh."

170. "A VIEW OF SNUG CORNER COVE, IN PRINCE WILLIAM'S SOUND." *May, 1778*
By John Webber, R.A., 22.3 x 36.6 cm., Watercolor.
DL, LNSW, Sydney, Australia.

This picture is duplicated in the British Museum; it was engraved by W. Ellis as Pl. XLV in the official account of the Third Voyage.

The expedition spent four days at this anchorage in the middle of May, repairing a bad leak that had developed in *Resolution*—as so often on the Third Voyage—because of her worn condition and skimped work in the naval shipyards. ". . . we gave the ship a good heel to port, in order to come at and stop the leak, on riping off the sheathing, it was found to be in the Seams which both in and under the wale, were very open and in several places not a bit of Oakam in them. . . . The 16th in the evening the weather cleared up when we found ourselves surrounded on every side by land; our Station was on the East side of the Sound in a place which in the Chart is distinguished by the name of Snug Corner bay, and a very snug place it is." It lies on the east side of Porcupine Point, almost at the entrance of the long inlet called Port Fidalgo.

Cook first named the Sound after Lord Sandwich, but later the name was changed to honor Prince William Henry, Duke of Clarence, afterwards William IV, the so-called "sailor King."

171. OUTSIDE THE HUTS AT UNALASCHKA,

N.W. Coast of America
William Ellis, Watercolor and ink. 9¾" x 13¼".
Rex Nan Kivell Collection, NLA, Canberra.

These northern scenes recorded by Ellis and Webber are of exceptional ethnographic interest and, despite the sublimity of view that would thoroughly have satisfied Edmund Burke, the mood is sombre, for one is looking at a harsh climate, stripped like the inhabitants to the barest essentials. But even so reduced the Indians and Eskimos somehow produce art of a form still universally admired. The huts are similar to the winter habitations of the Siberian coast entered by a notched ladder from a hole in the roof (see Kamchatka).

172. NATIVES OF THE ALEUTIAN ISLANDS, *1778*
Watercolor, pen and ink by John Webber. 12" x 19".
UWS (Edward W. Allen Collection), Seattle, Washington.

173. WALRUS, *1778* — Odobenus rosmarus
From a pencil and wash drawing signed: W. Ellis ad vivum del. et pinx. 1778. 19¼" x 24¼". NMG.

The drawing was made while *Resolution* was in the N.E. Pacific. William W. Ellis (d 1785) was assistant to the Surgeon's Mate, William Anderson, and acted also as natural history draughtsman for the Third Voyage.

The original is preserved in the British Museum (Natural History) Zoological Library.

174. SEA HORSES (*1778*)
Watercolor and pen and ink, John Webber. 17¼" x 24¾".
UWS (Edward W. Allen Collection), Seattle.

The "sea horses" provided good strong meat which the men needed and which they gladly took from the walrus. Unlike the sea beaver and other fur bearing animals, the walrus was hunted primarily for his ivory, and most of all by the natives who turned it into tools and great art.

175. SHOOTING WALRUSES, *1778*
Sea Horses
Engraving by E. Scott and J. Heath after J. Webber. Cook and King (1784), Pl. 52. 18½" x 23½". NMG, London.

Wednesday 19th (August, 1778) "On the ice lay a prodigious number of Sea horses and as we were in want of fresh provisions the boats from each ship were sent to get some . . . They lay in herds of many hundreds upon the ice, huddling one over the other like swine, and roar or bray very loud, so that in the night or foggy weather they gave us notice of the ice long before we could see it." Cook, Journal.

This engraving is derived from a rough but lively sketch, probably made on the spot by Webber and a wash drawing

177.

based on it which is equally vigorous (PAC *Paintings and Drawings and Prints,* 7110 and 7120). The large oil painting (49″ x 61½″) which he exhibited at the Royal Academy in 1784 is a highly finished work and, like the engraving, the scene is reversed. It now hangs in Admiralty House, Whitehall.

B. D. Smith, *European Vision and the South Pacific, 1768-1850,* Oxford, 1960.

176. INHABITANTS OF NORTON SOUND
Engraving after John Webber, Dr. Ira Pauly, Lake Oswego, Oregon.

This tinted engraving of the sere landscape of Norton Sound is more reminiscent of a woodland scene with luxuriant foliage of a Gainsborough park scene. However, the basics are there—a kayak and some salmon.

177. IN THE ARCTIC, *1778*
The RESOLUTION beating through the Ice, with the DISCOVERY in the most eminent danger in the distance. Aquatint after J. Webber (1752-93). Published April 1, 1809 by Boydell & Company. 21″ x 25″. NMG, London.

Cook was defeated by the ice in his search for a way around the north of America or Asia to the Atlantic and at times was in terrible danger of being trapped by the constantly shifting ice floes.

(18th August 1778) "We were at this time in 20 fathoms Water, close to the edge of the ice which was as compact as a Wall and seemed to be ten or twelve feet high as least . . . The *Discovery* being about a mile astern and to leeward found less water than we did and was obliged to tack for it . . . Our situation was now more and more critical, we were in shoald water upon a lee shore and the main body of the ice in sight to wind ward driving down upon us." Cook, Journal.

By good seamanship, Cook managed to extricate his ships from this position and sail clear of danger.

Aquatint from Webber, *Views in the South Seas,* 1808. The original watercolor is in the National Maritime Museum, Greenwich, with a second in the Peabody Museum of Harvard University, which places the scene as off Icy Cape, August 18, 1788.

178. HOW COOK DIED IN HAWAII, 14 FEBRUARY 1779
View of Owyhee, one of the Sandwich Islands in the South Seas, 1788. Aquatint by F. Jukes from John Cleveley (1747-86) after James Cleveley. 26″ x 32″. NMG, London, and Mariners' Museum, Newport News, Va.

Cook left Kealakekua Bay on 4 February 1779 with a sense of relief. As the days advanced the natives surrounding the anchorage had become less friendly, if not cool. Perhaps Cook was the great god Lono returned, but the villagers were also experiencing a shortage of food. It was apparent, too, that while Cook showed the manners of a god some of his followers did not. An older seaman had shown such human weakness as to die. It was disturbing.

As often happens along the Kona coast a sudden storm struck on the 6th and 7th, fracturing *Resolution's* foremast head. Perhaps Cook should have gone on, but the damage was grave and it was obvious there were few anchorages available to his ships. So the ships returned to the "safe anchorage" they had left on the 4th and found it relatively quiet.

While the repairs went forward Cook visited the shore again. All seemed serene, but *Resolution* was relatively helpless while her unstepped mast was repaired on shore. This must have exacerbated Cook, whose general disposition had weakened during the long voyage. Between his knowledge of the critical weakness of his flagship, the general health and morale of his men and the fluctuating adulation and hostility shown by the god-transfixed natives, Cook's once even temper was cruelly tested.

As in previous anchorages the natives went to all lengths to get metal from the intruders. It was for this reason that the important cutter was stolen from its *Discovery* moorage the night of 13 February. It was to be burned to get the iron fastenings. It was then that Cook resorted to earlier techniques to get the critical boat returned; he would go ashore and hold the old chief Terre'oboo captive until the boat was sent back. With a file of marines he set out in his boat accompanied by a pinnace piloted by Lieutenant Williamson whose crew was also heavily armed.

Walking a short distance inland to Terre'oboo's hut Cook persuaded the chief to accompany him to the rocky shore. The natives increased by the hundreds as Cook withdrew toward the shore with the genial chief and his waiting retinue. The crowd was alarmed and increasingly hostile as rumors spread of bloody events going on in their blockaded bay.

Although Cook was resolute and still in command, a melee developed which Samwell describes in his *Journal:* ". . . a Volley of Stones now came among our People on which the Marines gave a general fire and left themselves without a Reserve, this was instantly followed by a fire from the Boats, on which Capt. Cook . . . waved his hand to the Boats, told them to cease their fire and come nearer in to receive the People . . . no sooner had the Marines made their General Discharge but the body of them flung down their pieces and threw themselves into the water, on this all was over. The Indians immediately rushed down upon them, dragged those

who could not swim upon the Rocks where they dashed their brains out . . . Capt. Cook . . . was seen alive no more."

We know how rocky and uneven the lava flow is along this point. The sharp cliffs above were by description covered with frenzied natives, concerned for their aged leader and confused by the harsh actions of their New Year's god. The din must have been hair-raising, and Cook who had endured so much through the years may have momentarily broken when the now howling mob panicked his men. Then Cook fired a barrel of ineffectual bird shot . . . it rattled off harmlessly and emboldened the restive mob. The end came suddenly.

Blame was placed everywhere. But in the end it appeared as one of those needless and useless tragedies that riddle history. The loss of the ordinary marines and sailors was regrettable, but with Cook one pauses to muse, to reconsider and reflect. Cook had once written to the Admiralty: "I, who had the ambition not only to go farther than any man had ever been before, but as far as it was possible to go . . ." He had done all of that, and retirement to a sinecure in Greenwich Hospital may have been very far from his thoughts. Several views of his death are exhibited here, of which we believe only the James Cleveley eyewitness view to be reasonably accurate.

179. THE DEATH OF COOK, *14 February 1779*
Oil by John Zoffany, R.A. (1733-1810). 54″ x 72″.
NMG, London.

The Swiss emigré painter John Zoffany saw Cook in the contemporary manner as the ideal tragic hero of antiquity. Zoffany saw the elements of theatre and naturalism which were soon produced in a pantomime of masque entitled "The Death of Captain Cook: a grand Serious-Pantomimic Ballet . . . with the Original French music, new scenery, machinery, and Other Decorations." The tableau vivant ran in London and several provincial theatres, but unfortunately the music and stage directions have disappeared.

Zoffany had worked with David Garrick, the celebrated theatrical producer, and was also well-known to Sir Joseph Banks who invited him to join his retinue for the Second Voyage. After Banks withdrew in unrealistic pique Zoffany traveled to Italy while his patron went north to observe Iceland.

It is suggested that this portrait reveals how powerful the naturalistic element in painting had become, and the exceptional influence William Hodges had on the painters who came after him. The unusual feathered helmets favored by Hawaiian warriors of course proved ideal for the Zoffany relationship to a classical Greek theme, the death of Ludovasi Gladiator. This period is rich in studies of antiquity as stimulated by the

Duke of Hamilton in Naples, Lord Elgin in Greece and Charles Townley.

Zoffany had worked with William Hodges in India about 1783. In a six-year period there he must have absorbed much of the ailing master's experience and thoughts of the many exotic islands he had noted and sketched in naturalistic and experimental techniques.

180. THE DEATH OF CAPTAIN COOK, *1779*
By George Carter (1737-96). Oil painting on canvas.
NLA, Canberra, from the Rex Nan Kivell Collection.

Another oil painting, of the same subject, also attributed to Carter, is owned by the Bernice P. Bishop Museum, Honolulu. The only scene illustrating Cook's death, made by an eyewitness, was by James Cleveley; the aquatint after his brother John is exhibited together with an engraving after Webber's oil of the event (often published) and the oil painting by Zoffany—all but Cleveley's are reconstructions of the occurrences. No such action by Cook, as shown by Carter, is recorded.

181. THE DEATH OF CAPTAIN COOK, SUNDAY, 14 FEBRUARY 1779, AT KEALAKEKUA BAY, HAWAII
By F. Jukes from a watercolor drawing by John Cleveley after a sketch by James Cleveley. 16.7 x 23.6 cm., aquatint hand-finished in color. MM, Newport News, Virginia.

Published in 1788 as one of a set of four such aquatints, the scene is titled: "View of Owyhee, one of the Sandwich Islands in the South Seas." It is of especial interest as being probably the most accurate of several representations of Cook's death. There are some versions of these aquatints in sepia, and there was a French edition.

James Cleveley (fl 1776-80) was a carpenter in *Resolution*, the youngest son of a family of artists, but apparently untrained. His elder brother John Cleveley (1767-86) was a talented artist, who was long in the employ of Joseph Banks. After James returned from the Third Voyage, John worked up some of his drawings into watercolors, of which only six seem to remain. Beaglehole, assisted by the investigations of Miss Phyllis Mander Jones, sometime Mitchell Librarian, reached the conclusion that probably only two of the sketches made by James have survived (in London) and that color may have been added to them by John.

Although Webber did not witness Cook's death, he also made a painting of it, probably based upon Cleveley's version very largely, but reversed. A large engraving after Webber, with the figures done by Bartolozzi and the landscape by W. Byrne, was published in 1786, and a smaller issue of it is

DESIGN·FOR·A·NATIONAL·MONUMENT·TO·THE·MEMORY·OF
CAPTAIN·COOK
BY·THOMAS·BANKS·SCULPTOR
CAPTAIN·COOK·IS·REPRESENTED·DEAD·ON·A·GLOBE
THE·GENII·CASTOR·AND·POLLUX·OR·THE·MARINERS·GUIDE
POINT·OUT·ON·THE·GLOBE·THE·LATITUDE·HE·SAILD·TO·AND·THE
SPOT·WHERE·HE·LOST·HIS·LIFE
BRITANNIA·IS·ERECTING·A·TROPHY

183.

CIRCA ORBEM

NIL INTENTATUM RELIQUIT

The Armorial Bearings of
CAPTAIN JAMES COOK, R.N.,
as Recorded at
the College of Arms, London
Conrad Swan
York
York Herald of Arms

184.

185.

often bound in with Third Voyage plates. He painted several oils of it, one being in the Dixson Library, Sydney. George Carter and the romantic classicist, Zoffany, made their own interpretations also on view in this exhibition.

Two young men who performed poorly that Sunday morning were William Bligh, Master of *Resolution* at 21(!) and Lt. John Williamson. Bligh much too aggressively blocked egress from the Bay while the secretive Williamson was in charge of the pinnace which accompanied Cook's landing party In the melee the pinnace and cutter closed the shore to rescue panicked men, but not so Williamson. He was subsequently even more despised. Twelve years later both were Captains at bloody Camperdown, Bligh in *Director* (64) one of the noble Duncan's best, and Williamson in *Agincourt* (64). Each performed unevenly. *Agincourt* failed to support Captain Burgess in *Ardent* (64) and ill-fated Williamson, courtmartialed for cowardice, disaffection and negligence, was sentenced in the latter count—never to serve again. Admiral Duncan, all 6 feet 4 inches of him, was made a viscount.

182. APOTHEOSIS OF COOK
Wouvermann engraving. 8½″ x 10½″. ATL, Wellington, N.Z.

This rich conception in its attractive excessiveness and beautifully defined lines reveals the fact that the end of the Age of Reason is at hand. The simple thought in this rather conventional conception is strikingly opposite from any aspect of Cook's rather rational Scottish thinking, which clearly did not include a heralding angel on a celestial voyage, or, possibly, grieving Britannia and her laurel wreath.

183. DESIGN FOR A NATIONAL MONUMENT TO THE MEMORY OF CAPTAIN COOK
By Thomas Banks, sculptor. 9″ x 13″. ATL, Wellington, N.Z.

One can almost wonder that at the end of his career Cook should again come up against a man named Banks, another very involved mind as one can see from the deeply engrossed Castor and Pollux. Happily for Cook this massive and miscalculated memorial was, unlike so many others as the new century presented itself, not built. Britannia was busy elsewhere.

To be preferred is the conception of Cook looking off over the still perilous entrance to Whitby harbor, an early challenge, or into the hurrying streets of London, Wellington or other cities throughout the world. There are over 200 monuments to Cook around the world he charted.

184. COAT-OF-ARMS BESTOWED IN SEPTEMBER, 1885 POSTHUMOUSLY ON JAMES COOK, POST-CAPTAIN IN THE ROYAL NAVY (1728-79),

by His Majesty King George III of England.
Watercolors on vellum, ATL, Wellington, N.Z.

As the first step toward nobility, the right to bear arms was a jealously guarded privilege. It is believed that Cook's Arms were the last ever bestowed in Great Britain for personal service to the Sovereign, reflecting the King's admiration for Cook. Had Cook returned from the Third Voyage, he would surely have been knighted as Sir James, and would have been promoted to the rank of Admiral of the White in the Royal Navy.

An azure shield carries two golden "polar stars": between them, on a map of the Pacific hemisphere, are marked in scarlet the tracks of Cook's voyages, terminating at Hawaii. The heraldic description runs: "Azure between two polar stars Or, a sphere on the plane of the meridian, shewing the Pacific Ocean, his track thereon marked by red lines. And for crest, on a wreath of the colours, is an arm bowed, in the uniform of a Captain of the Royal Navy. In the hand is the Union Jack on a staff proper. The arm is encircled by a wreath of palm and laurel."

The use of two Latin mottoes is most unusual, but both are extremely well-chosen, for *Circa orbem* (placed above the crest) may be translated as "Around the Globe," and *Nil intentatum reliquit* (below the shield) as "He left nothing unattempted." Cook himself wrote, in the Antarctic waters on the Second Voyage (of more than 60,000 miles): "I whose ambition leads me not only further than any other man has been before me, but as far as I think it possible for man to go . . ."

This rare example of Cook's own Coat-of-arms was prepared by the York Herald of Arms, London, for the National Film Unit of New Zealand in 1968, for use in a full-length Cook Bicentennial film of 1969. It was presented to the Alexander Turnbull Library in 1970.

185. A VIEW OF THE TOWN AND HARBOR OF ST. PETER AND ST. PAUL, KAMCHATKA
John Webber, Watercolor. 28½″ x 20¾″.
LNSW, Sydney, Australia.

This is an exceptional view showing not only the huddle of the village of Petropavlovsk, but also the important sand bar intruding into the harbor behind which the town nestles. This bar where we believe Clerke's first burial took place was also the scene of the Russian protective screen when the Anglo-French flotilla unsuccessfully attacked the strategic harbor during the Crimean War. These cool northern colors are far removed from the brilliant coloration of Hodges' brush.

Ia. M. Svet, "Novye dannye o prebyvanii na Kamchatka

187.

tret'eu exspeditsii Dzhemsa Kuka" (1779g) *Novoe v Izucheii Avstralii I Okeanii (Sborniic Statlei).*

186. BALAGANS OR SUMMER HABITATIONS WITH THE METHOD OF DRYING FISH AT ST. PETER ET PAUL, KAMTSCHATKA

John Webber, Watercolor and ink. 14¼″ x 19¼″.
Rex Nan Kivell Collection, NLA, Canberra.

This historic harbor in the bay of Avatcha is one of the great harbors of the world, and first achieved fame as the staging area for Vitus Bering's great expedition a generation before Cook. The harbor, which freezes solid in winter, was named for his two ships *St. Peter* and *St. Paul*. As we can see, salmon was a staple in the diet of the Cossacks and Kamchadals in the village. The balagans provide some relief from the summer swarming insects and half-starved sled dogs—that would eat the harness and leather finished tools.

187. POLAR BEAR, *Kamchatka, 1779. A White Bear Engraved by Mazell after J. Webber (1752-93), 16½″ x 18″.* NMG, London.

The original watercolor by Webber (National Library of Australia NK52A) was faithfully copied by the engraver, but the impression shows the bear reversed.

Engraving from Cook & King (1784), Pl. 73.

188. VIEW ON THE ISLAND OF PULO CONDORE

John Webber, Watercolor and pen. 14¼″ x 19¼″.
Rex Nan Kivell Collection, NLA, Canberra.

After leaving Macao and Canton on the final voyage home under Gore, the ships stopped for a week in the China Sea at the above pictured high island. There the expedition bought buffalo meat, caught fish, and took on fresh water.

189. VIEW ON THE ISLAND OF CRACATOA

John Webber, Watercolor and pen, 14½″ x 19½″.
Rex Nan Kivell Collection, NLA, Canberra.

Sailing toward Capetown Commodore Gore stopped briefly in Krakatoa in the Sunda Strait which was visited by a giant eruption and earthquake roughly a century later. The broken crater had erupted in 1680, then in 1877 the area was subjected to earthquakes. From May through August eruptions occurred. On August 27 giant explosions shook the East Indies, and Batavia, 100 miles away, was covered with ash as stones and debris shot 17 miles into the air above the fragmenting volcano.

The sound was heard at Rodrigues (3,000 miles away!) and the tsunami shock waves developed traveled 7,800 miles to Cape Horn, and perhaps to the English Channel. Thirty-six thousand people died in Krakatoa's convulsions. This is just a brief idea of the kind of tremor the casually named Pacific is known to produce in its troubled periods.

190. THE FAN PALM, IN THE ISLAND OF CRACATOA, *1780*

Aquatint by J. Webber, 1788. Published April 1st, 1809 by Boydell & Company. From Webber, VIEWS IN THE SOUTH SEAS, London (1808), Pl. 16. 25″ x 20″. NMG, London.

From Kamchatka, the ships made their way homeward by way of the east coast of Japan, Macao and the Sunda Strait and so to the Cape of Good Hope. In February, 1780, at the island of Krakatoa, in the Strait, they watered ship. The fan palm impressed the visitors because it provided a refreshing drink, a sweet syrup and was used to thatch houses, make baskets, cups, umbrellas and tobacco pipes.

Webber, like Hodges, was attempting to combine anatomical exactitude (scientific observation) with the general effect (artistic sensibility) in his paintings, to blend instead of to separate the two cultures already becoming distinct—science and the humanities—in the closing years of the 18th century. In the event, the influence of Webber and Hodges prevailed and we still seek to blend where possible.

Webber himself engraved and published the original aquatint, 1 August 1788.

191. SILVER-HANDLED KNIFE AND TWO-PRONGED FORK, *said to have been Captain Cook's on the Third Voyage, 1776-80, ATL, Wellington, N.Z.*

These were purchased about 1830 by the Hon. William B. Rhodes, from Maoris in the Marlborough Sound who claimed they had been Cook's. His utensils would have been like these, but it is possible these belonged to Captain Clerke or another officer who was with Cook at Queen Charlotte Sound about 50 years before. There is no other likely source, and we know the many complaints about pilferage. They were bequeathed to the Library in 1961 by a descendant of Captain Barnard Rhodes, the late William Dubois Ferguson, Esq.

192. AMMUNITION BELT, OF LEATHER, WITH SEPARATE POUCHES FOR CARRYING POWDER, SHOT AND BALL. *Ownership attributed to COOK. ML, LNSW, Sydney, Australia.*

When Cook was killed at Hawaii, he first fired his musket ineffectually, one barrel of which was loaded with bird shot, the second with a ball. The Mitchell Library gives J. Mackrell as the source of the belt, which was transferred to the Library from the Australian Museum in October, 1955.

193. WAR CLUB FROM TONGAN OR

195.

200.

FRIENDLY ISLANDS

Reputed to have been collected by William Griffin (1755-1839), cooper of the RESOLUTION during the Third Voyage (1776-80). NMG.

Wednesday 16th (July, 1777) "Many people likewise fought with clubs of the hard heavy Cocoa nut stem, a diversion I think the most exceptional they have, both because it is in some degree cruel and requires no dexterity so that the advantage must generally be on the side of strength . . ." Anderson, Journal.

194. TONGAN WAR CLUB, 1777
CAM, Cambridge, England.

This powerful design of a hardwood Tonganese war club (length 100.4 cm., circumference 21.5 cm.) is in magnificent condition. While it has evidently seen more use than No. 111, it also shows less complex design and skilled execution, although it is from the Third Voyage. The fine workmanship very likely has no relationship to any "traumatic" acculturation; the design and the club itself could likely be much earlier than the 1770s and also more of a business piece than the more elaborate version.

195. THROWING CLUB, FIJI
NMG, London.

This Ula, or throwing club, is supposed to have been brought home from the Third Voyage.

196. BREADFRUIT POUNDER, TAHITI
NMG, London.

This Poi, or breadfruit pounder used in Tahiti, was brought home on the Third Voyage (1776-80).

197. BARK CLOTH OR TAPA FROM THE SOUTH SEAS
NMG, London.

The roll exhibited here, although of a later date than the Cook voyages, was made in the same manner that Cook described so well in his Journal for the First Voyage, when at Tahiti, July, 1769.

". . . all their cloth is . . . made from the bark of trees, the finest is from a plant which they cultivate for no other purpose . . . they cut it down and lay it a certain time in water, this makes the bark strip easy off, the outside of which is then scraped off with a rough shell, after this is done it looks like long strips of raged linen. These they lay together, by means of a fine paste made of some sort of root [the starchy pia] to the breadth of a yard or more or less and in length Six, Eight or ten yards or more according to the use it is for, after it is thus put together it is beat out to its proper breadth and fineness upon a long, square piece of wood with wooden beaters the cloth being Kept wet all the time . . . Thick cloth especially fine is made by pasting two or more thickness's of thin cloth made for that purpose together . . . their common colors are red, brown and yellow with which they dye some pieces just as their fancy leads them . . ."

198. TAPA CLOTH SAMPLES COLLECTED BY COOK IN THE SOUTH PACIFIC ISLANDS
APL (remounted) and ATL (as published).

Published as a book in 1787, these rare volumes have a title page reading: "*A Catalogue of the Different Specimens of Cloth Collected in the Three Voyages of Captain Cook, to the Southern Hemisphere . . . partly extracted from Mr. Anderson and Reinhold Forster's observations . . . with some anecdotes that happened to them among the natives. Now properly arranged and printed for Alexander Shaw, No. 379, Strand, London, MDCCLXXXVII.*"

Each copy varies slightly in its specimens and their number.

199. FLY FLAP, SANDWICH ISLANDS
NMG, London.

Fly whisk of cocoanut fibre, mounted on a handle formed from a spear point of a type used in the Sandwich Islands. It was brought home from the Third Voyage (1776-80).

200. CONICAL STRAW HAT, N.W. Coast America
Diameter 28 cm., height 24 cm., circumference 89 cm. NMI, Dublin, Ireland.

The pear-shaped bulb surmounting this almost perfect conical hat of fern stem and grasses was brought back by James King, and eventually deposited in Dublin. Brown in color with designs of whales and canoes, this rare artifact from King George's Sound (Nootka) uses a wrapped twining technique to form the hat. The bulb was a typical decorative device of that period.

201. DEER'S HOOF BRACELET (*Nootka Sound*)
NMI, Dublin, Ireland.

A beautiful stylized ornament which indicates in the purest kind of design why Northwest Coast pieces have held such interest from the first incident of European contact. As in every case, however, even the strongest design elements changed immediately upon the arrival of Cook's ships and those of other Pacific explorers and traders.

202. WHALEBONE CLUB, N. W. COAST AMERICA
Vancouver's Voyage (1791-95), CAM.
Length 58.5 cm., width 7.5 cm.

207.

203.

206.

Vancouver sailed with Cook on the last two voyages and forever after Cook was regarded as the master by this second great surveyor.

One of the most impressive facts recorded was the technique by which the Northwest Coast tribes took whales, sharks, and large fish from the ocean. This club is a repeat of those brought back by Cook's sailors. A lenticular cross section is surmounted by a bird head with head dress, circular eye insert of abalone, and a distinctive triangular motif along one central ornamental line.

203. BEAVER BOWL. *Nootka—Third Voyage*
13″ x 7″ x 2″. NMG, London.

This superb wooden bowl carved with a curved tail and head to represent a beaver may have been traded during the long March stay at Nootka Sound (1778). While this is not known for certain the attribution is reasonably sound, since it was brought home on the Third Voyage (1776-80).

Beaver furs remained in importance as a trade item although they were immediately overshadowed by the luxuriant sea otter pelts. The beaver was familiar, the exotic sea otter was not.

204. HARDWOOD CLUB, *Hawaii*
Length 32 cm., width 7 cm. LEN, 505-5, USSR.

This wood and shark tooth club from the Captain Cook Collection in Leningrad reveals the simple level of armaments among the Hawaiians. Despite their many inter-island wars only the most neolithic simple weaponry had been developed. All Russian pieces are from the Museum of Anthropology and Ethnography; received 1780.

205. DANCING BATON *62 cm. overall*
LEN, Museum of Anthropology and Ethnography, 505-6, USSR.

When Cook and his ship moved in toward the Islands, Gore went ashore. Immediately apparent was the fact that the Hawaiian natives had developed few weapons. They were more apt to have dancing rods such as this one from the Third Voyage, rather than clubs. Decorated with white dog's tail.

206. FEATHER CAPE, *Hawaii*
From the Third Voyage. Length at cloak breast, 23 cm.; at outside edge, 174 cm. LEN, 505-19, USSR.

As Heinrich Zimmerman stated (*Reise um die Welt mit Capitain Cook*, Mannheim, 1781): "Rarely did we see either the king or the chief at any other time wearing their red cloaks or caps . . .* These red cloaks are made with great care. The inside of the cloak usually consists of a mat of plaited grass and the outside is covered over richly with small red feathers

which are mixed with even rows of black, yellow, and green feathers, the colors standing out well from each other. These garments were universally acknowledged to be the most beautiful and artistic rarities which had been met with among the native peoples visited."

This is one of three owned by the Museum of Ethnography, Leningrad, the old Museum of Curiosities founded by Peter the Great. It is from the ethnographical treasure saved through the action of Premier Major Magnus von Boehm, who succored the Cook expedition on its last voyage north during which journey gallant Clerke stopped twice in Petropavlovsk, the last time to be buried after his death from tuberculosis. As Zimmerman reports of Behm (or Boehm): ". . . a written report of Captain Cook's death was entrusted to Governor Boehm who had just been recalled to St. Petersburg, and who would therefore reach Europe before us . . . *Some presents of objects of natural history were also sent for his Majesty, the Russian Emperor*" (sic) (author's italics). They are elsewhere mentioned as "trifles" (King). See also letter attachment Major von Behm, 16 September 1779 by F. N. Klitcka, Governor of Irkutsk to General Procurator A. A. Vjazemskiy. Also, letter 29 May 1780, F. N. Klitcka to Vjazemskiy with attachment of Captain V. I. Shmalev concerning the second arrival of Cook's ships at Petropavlovsk.
*Tr. Miss U. Tensley, Alexander Turnbull Library (Bull. No. 2, 1926).

207. A WOMAN'S ORNAMENT
LEN, 505-13, USSR.

Wherever the Cook voyagers penetrated, the women of the islands or continental littorals wore some kind of adornment, simple or ingenious and intricate.

In describing these in some detail the Cook recorders, including the tireless navigator himself, made exceptional and early contributions to ethnography. All of the Leningrad pieces shown, including these "wild boar fangs," were accessioned in St. Petersburg in 1780 from the Cook expedition.

208. CHEST SHIELD, *Tahiti*
Diameter 45 cm., width 16 cm. LEN, 505-14, USSR.

When beleaguered Cook fired his ineffectual barrel of bird shot into the melee the results were catastrophic. The shot rattled off a chest shield and emboldened the crowd. Having earlier seen the stout body armor (chest shields) of the Northwest Coast one would think that the Captain might have immediately used ball rather than shot. But he had also seen the frail "taomes" of Tahiti which were constructed of palm twigs and coir. This rare example of taome, decorated with shark's teeth, feathers and dog's hair, was made for a chief.

208.

209.

211.

212.

It was not made to resist firearms.

209. BAG, TONGA ISLANDS, POLYNESIA
Length 34 cm., width 43 cm. LEN, 505-32, USSR.

A woman's bag (?) composed of coir, grass and white shell beads.

210. FISHING HOOKS
Lengths 8 and 8.5 cm.; thicknesses 1.2 and 0.4 cm.
LEN, 505-25, 505-26, USSR.

Wherever the expeditions landed the natives encountered were dependent upon fish as part of their basic diet. In some cases a more elaborate net and weir technique was encountered, especially along the rocky river-fed inlets of the North American coast and Siberia. Huge cyclical runs of salmon were part of the food pattern of the northerly tribes, along with shell and rock fish and deep sea fisheries.

The native gear in the southerly regions was fashioned of shell or rock, sometimes barbed, though not always, with ingenious carving to represent a fish or part of one, especially fashioned in mother-of-pearl. These from Hawaii and Polynesia are tortoise shell. Northwest Coast abalone shell was used and a more highly developed and lethal ivory and barbed bone construction for very large fish as well as fur bearing aquatic animals.

See "Die Sudsee-und Alaskasammlung Johan Waber Beschreibender Katalog," Karl H. Heinking, in *Jahrbuch des Bernischen Historischen Museums, Vol. XXXV and XXXVL* (1955-56).

211. POLYNESIAN PILLOW-STOOL
Palmwood or mahogany. Length 52 cm., height 12 cm.
LEN, 505-1, USSR.

The utility of this simple but beautifully designed piece of furniture for night and day use reveals why the same style prevails in Micronesia today.

212. AXE-ADZE
LEN, 505-28, Leningrad, USSR.

The Nootka or Wakashians were well acquainted with iron and had a quantity of it on hand for weapons and tools before Cook appeared. But they were eager for brass or copper although they had their own copper from beaches and ledges. They also secured chance amounts of drift iron which landed on the beaches of the North Pacific.

The natives used iron in their axes as well as sharp stone, slate, or argillite. The Hawaiians however had no metal and relied on hardwood and stone axes as well as wooden daggers and spears and stones. The helve is wood (54 cm.) with a black basalt blade (21.5 cm. length, width 5.2 cm.).

213. WOODEN DAGGER
Length 49 cm. LEN, 505-33, USSR.

A hard wood dagger, showing again the development of weaponry among the stone age peoples. Samwell noted Hawaiian daggers "of fine polished black wood," in February, 1779.

The interesting aspect is how swiftly and singlemindedly all natives fastened upon metal (iron, brass, copper, lead, etc.) and its uses including the forging of iron. No doubt they observed the *Resolution's* armorer at work on the rudder taken ashore the end of January, 1779, when he had to "fix Iron hoops over the head piece . . ." They were soon firing iron and bending it by pounding on the lava rocks.

214. KNIFE OR DAGGER OF MONKEY POD WOOD AND SHARK'S TOOTH
CAM E 1920.803, England.

An examination of this superb serrated shark tooth knife with edged hardwood blade from the Sandwich Islands immediately reveals why the natives were "inclined to thieving & that Iron was their principal Object." Cook Journal January 18, 1778.

Trade began with nails and in time the armorers were making long daggers of a kind used to stab Cook in the neck.

215. BOAR TUSKS BRACELET, *Sandwich Islands*
CAM Z 611F, England.

This fine ornamental bracelet of 19 matched tusks, a kupp-hoakalakala, acquired on the Third Voyage in Hawaii, is the duplicate of that held by the Museo Nazionale di Antropologia e Etnologia in Florence, Italy, even to the number of tusks.

Reprise

I want to acknowledge the generous manner in which almost every museum and private collection responded to our inquiries and questions. In some cases, most in fact, the response was to say the least remarkable. One or two are somewhat moribund obviously, or seriously understaffed. Others wished very much to participate, but were simply unable to do so due to the rigid policies of their trustees, war losses, general deterioration, and other stresses of time: for example, Glasgow, Newcastle, and Capetown, the Bishop Museum (Honolulu), Berlin and Gottingen. Berlin and Vienna wished to cooperate. This was true also in reference to Bern and Florence

One can certainly understand their decisions, especially in reference to such fragile examples as feather-work, the finest of which I have seen in Leningrad. Such do not travel well and the responsibility in the last analysis is really too much, attractive as the vision is.

To know where the artifacts of Cook's voyages traveled is to know almost every great ethnographic holding in Europe. The person who knows this best is probably Adrienne Kaeppler, presently with the Bishop Museum in Honolulu.

I want also to mention those museums such as Cambridge University and the Museum of Anthropology and Ethnography in Leningrad which immediately made extraordinary efforts to cooperate in a generous way. This was appreciated more than I can say by my colleagues and me.

To every museum curator who participated in one way or another this Society is most grateful, and we regret the one or two who addressed in their own language on more than one occasion failed to reply.

Thomas Vaughan

Contributors to the Cook Exhibition
Leo Adler
Anonymous
Autzen Foundation
Mrs. Clarence M. Bishop
John W. Blodgett, Jr.
Mr. and Mrs. Clarence A. Chase
Julian N. Cheatham Foundation
Delta Kappa Gamma — Theta Chapter
Miss Elizabeth C. Ducey
Flowerree Foundation
Kenneth W. Ford Foundation
Dr. and Mrs. Donald E. Forster
W. Burns Hoffman
Joseph A. Minott
Mr. and Mrs. John W. S. Platt
O. C. Roehr
Mary Alice Rulifson
Mrs. Paul Stark Seeley
Mrs. Laurence Selling
Mr. and Mrs. Laurence L. Shaw
Mrs. John A. Sprouse
Mrs. Donald J. Sterling, Sr.
Swindells Foundation
Mr. and Mrs. Moe M. Tonkon
James D. Tredup
United States National Bank of Oregon

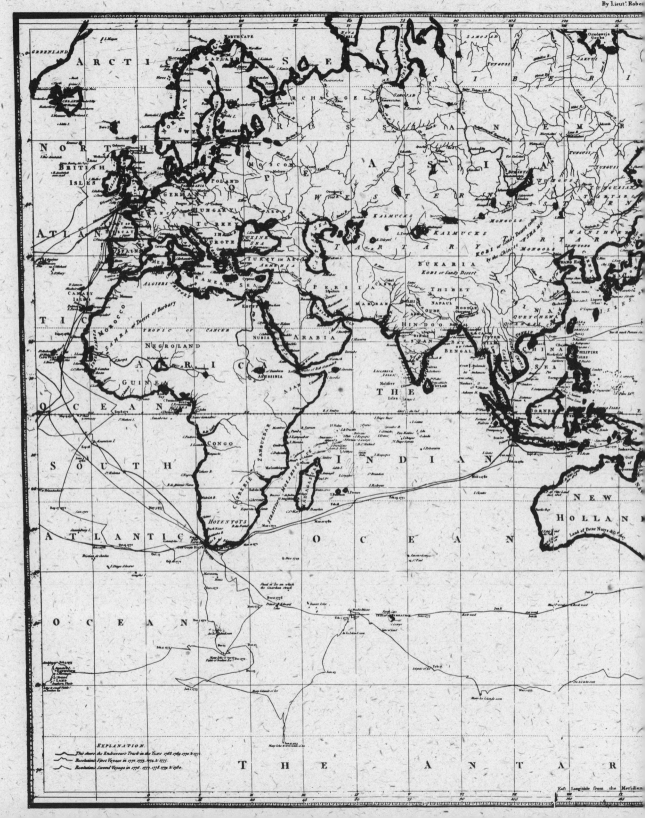

GREENLAND

ARCTI   S E A

NORTH CAPE   NOVA
LAPLAND   SAMOJAD   Omolowaja
                                        SIBERI   Gora
        SWEDEN   JAKUTI
NORWAY   ARCHANGEL
                                TUNGUSI

NORTH   MOSCOW   SIBERI
BRITISH   R
ISLES   POLAND   TUNGUSI
        GERMANY   RUSSIA   Orenburg   TUNGUSI
ATLAN   HUNGARY   DON R.   KALMUCKS   MANSHU
        FRANCE   TARTARY
        TURKEY   BLACK   KALMUCKS   Kobi or Sandy Desert called   MONGOLS
        IN   SEA   by the Chinese SHAMO
        EUROPE   ARMENIA   TARTARY   MONGOLS   HANG HO
MEDITERRANEAN   Cyprus   CASPIAN SEA   BUKARIA
ALGIERS   SEA   Kobi or Sandy Desert   THIBET   CHINA
MOROCCO   PERSIA   NAPAUL   QUETCHEW
SAHRA or Desert of Barbary   Ispahan   MAKRAN   ROOTAN   QUAN SI
        TROPIC OF CANCER   NUBIA   ARABIA   HINDOO   CHINA
NEGROLAND   STAN   BAY of   SEA
        A F R I C A   ABYSSINIA   MALDIVE   BENGAL   PHILIPINE
                                LACCADIVE   Isles   ISLES
GUINEA   AJAN   ISLES   CEYLON
                        THE   BORNEO
OCEAN   CONGO   ZANGUEBAR   INDIAN
        St. Helena   MADAGASCAR   NEW
SOUTH   Ascension I.   HOLLAND
        ATLANTIC   HOTENTOTS   Cape of Good Hope   OCEAN
                                Land of Peter Nuyts dis. 1627
OCEAN   INDIAN   OCEAN

        OCEAN

EXPLANATION.
This shews the Endeavours Track in the Years 1768. 1769. 1770 & 1771.
Resolution's First Voyage in 1772. 1773. 1774. & 1775.
Resolution's Second Voyage in 1776. 1777. 1778. 1779. & 1780.